GET LIT RISING

RISING

WORDS IGNITE. CLAIM YOUR POEM. CLAIM YOUR LIFE.

DIANE LUBY LANE AND THE GET LIT PLAYERS

Simon Pulse
New York London Toronto Sydney New Delhi

 BEYOND WORDS
Hillsboro, Oregon

SIMON PULSE

An imprint of Simon & Schuster, Inc.
Children's Publishing Division
1230 Avenue of the Americas
New York, NY 10020

BEYOND WORDS
20827 N.W. Cornell Road, Suite 500
Hillsboro, Oregon 97124-9808
503-531-8700 / 503-531-8773 fax
www.beyondword.com

This Beyond Words/Simon Pulse edition October 2016
Compilation copyright © 2016 by Get Lit—Words Ignite, Inc.
Cover copyright © 2016 by Beyond Words/Simon & Schuster, Inc.

SIMON PULSE and colophon are registered trademarks of Simon & Schuster, Inc.

Beyond Words is an imprint of Simon & Schuster, Inc., and the Beyond Words logo is a registered trademark of Beyond Words Publishing, Inc.

Managing Editor: Lindsay S. Easterbrooks-Brown
Copyeditors: Jennifer Weaver-Neist, Emmalisa Sparrow
Cover design: Sara E. Blum
Interior design: Devon Smith
Photographer: Daniel Sawyer Schaefer
Composition: William H. Brunson Typography Services
The text of this book was set in Arno Pro and Felt Tip.

For information about special discounts for bulk purchases, please contact Simon & Schuster Special Sales at 1-866-506-1949 or business@simonandschuster.com.

The Simon & Schuster Speakers Bureau can bring authors to your live event. For more information or to book an event contact the Simon & Schuster Speakers Bureau at 1-866-248-3049 or visit our website at www.simonspeakers.com.

Manufactured in the United States of America

10 9 8 7 6 5 4 3 2 1

Library of Congress Cataloging-in-Publication Data

Names: Lane, Diane Luby, author, editor. | Get Lit Players, author.
  Title: Get lit rising : Words ignite. Claim your poem. Claim your life. /
    Diane Luby Lane and the Get Lit Players.
  Description: New York : Simon Pulse/Beyond Words, 2016.
  Identifiers: LCCN 2015046398 (print) | LCCN 2016007076 (ebook) |
    ISBN 9781582705767 (hardback) | ISBN 9781582705774 (paperback) |
    ISBN 9781481457200 (eBook)
  Subjects: LCSH: Poetry—Juvenile literature. | Poetry—Authorship—Juvenile
    literature. | American poetry—21st century. | Poets, American—21st
    century—Biography—Juvenile literature. | American poetry—21st
    century—History and criticism—Juvenile literature. | Children's poetry,
    American. | BISAC: JUVENILE NONFICTION / Poetry / General. | JUVENILE
    NONFICTION / Biography & Autobiography / Performing Arts. | JUVENILE
    NONFICTION / Language Arts / Composition & Creative Writing.
  Classification: LCC PN1031 .G456 2016 (print) | LCC PN1031 (ebook) |
    DDC 808.1—dc23

LC record available at http://lccn.loc.gov/2015046398

FOR VIVECA LINDFORS AND EVERY SOUL
WHO DARES TO MAKE A DIFFERENCE.

PROCEEDS FROM THE SALES OF THIS BOOK GO DIRECTLY
TO THE OUTREACH PROGRAMS AT

It is important that I tell you their names…
—Ta-Nehisi Coates

CONTENTS

FOREWORD

BY TiM ROBBINS

I grew up at a time and in a place where art was flourishing. My public school education in New York City provided classes devoted to visual, mechanical, and theatrical arts. It was a requirement to learn a musical instrument. Poetry was a key component in our study of English.

As we progressed into the '80s and '90s, however, the troglodytes setting policy and making budgets began the slow decline and ultimate decimation of funding for arts education in our public schools. As this money disappeared, dropout rates increased. As dropout rates increased, crime rates rose. As crime rates rose, more prisons were built. We criminalized more and more nonviolent offenses, and our jails were soon full of young men and women who had fallen from the margins of society into a web of incarceration. In the last twenty years, twenty-two prisons were built in the state of California and, in that same time, only two universities. In my work inside prisons, I regularly encounter the results of our failed education policy. Anecdotally, I can tell you that roughly 80 percent of those incarcerated had little to no arts education in their public schools.

So is there a connection between our education policy and our incarceration rate? Undoubtedly. Ask any child lucky enough to be involved with arts programs. Ask the kids at Get Lit or Inner-City Arts or in programs we run at the Actors' Gang. The arts are a lifeline for children with learning difficulties or those not gifted with mathematical brains or those who, try as they will, can't get excited about the periodic table.

My access to the arts as a freshman and as a sophomore in high school was the only reason I had any enthusiasm to go to school. I was lost in other subjects. My brain wasn't made that way. Was I stigmatized? No. I had teachers who understood that I was not on my way to a career in physics and encouraged the talents that I did possess. One of them, an English teacher named Thomas Dolan, got me involved in theater. Today, Tom Dolan would probably not have a job.

Depriving our children of the arts—a passion that may keep them interested in their own education—is, in essence, giving up on those children. It is basically eliminating the sole reason that many of those children may have to stay involved with their education. Our current education policy is not only detrimental to a child's education; it is also a threat to the safety and health of society at large.

I have personally seen and met with hundreds of children whose lives have been turned around by art. Most inspiring have been the teen poets from Get Lit, who, through their involvement with this organization, have reignited their commitment to their own education. It wasn't the government that made this happen. It was the passion and belief of one individual, a young mother and actress named Diane Luby Lane, who made Get Lit happen. It was her vision and her relentless pursuit of funding for her vision that created an outlet to inspire the kids that our schools had left behind.

And inspire she did. Not only the children who became part of Get Lit but also everyone who has heard the words that have come out of these young poets' souls. I have sat at the monthly Get Lit poetry slams at the

Actors' Gang theater and have witnessed lives transformed by art. I have heard passionate and talented young artists testify their truth. I have seen the shy and intimidated become strong and empowered. I have wept at the profound effect that words can have on all of us and have been reminded of the purpose and mission of poetry itself. I have seen young poets from Get Lit go from alienated youth to college-bound scholarship students.

It doesn't take much. It takes individuals like Diane. She held a light out so that they could find their way. This essential light that Get Lit provides gives children an illuminated path away from gangs and the fast track to the prison system that is all too prevalent in the United States.

I hope someday the troglodytes figure out the connection between the arts and public safety. When our leaders finally understand that arts education is an essential and necessary part of a child's development— when comprehensive arts programs are provided that leave no child behind—let us have the grace and empathy to applaud our leaders for their vision and forward-thinking policy. This change must happen. It is essential if we want a future where the United States doesn't lead the world in incarceration rates.

But until then, it is Diane and the warriors at Get Lit whose good efforts, hard work, and commitment to poetic literacy will create a brighter future. It is the teachers like Thomas Dolan and the volunteers who have the vision to see the individual within the child as essential— people who put in unpaid time to point those kids in a direction that is good for who they are and who they can become, rather than crippling them with the expectation of curriculums that choke them. Soon we will understand as a society that holding up a light for one child is not enough. It is our civic responsibility to see to it that every child has the capacity and the confidence to light their own path, leaving us stunned, inspired, and applauding in their wake.

Tim Robbins is an Academy Award–winning actor/writer/director and the founder of the Actors' Gang and the Actors' Gang Prison Project.

FOREWORD

BY LUIS J. RODRIGUEZ

In a world where Bill O'Reilly gets to yell on TV for ideals without facts, Judge Judy disrespects defendants as if having a black robe makes her immune from basic human decorum, and Ann Coulter can claim Anglo culture is the most cultured, where are the voices that speak out for all our humanity, in all its complexities, flavors, colors, tongues, practices, and stories?

One place for sure is among the young people, teachers, and mentors of Get Lit Players in Los Angeles. This is a city where guns can be obtained by anybody in any neighborhood, but books cannot be bought for miles across South and East LA and the northeast San Fernando Valley.

This is a city that provides 60 percent of the state's massive prison system—at $10 billion a year with 140,000 prisoners—and has the nation's largest homeless population. Yet LA also has some of the highest-priced homes and office buildings in the world. Where you can enjoy foods from everywhere—Mexico, Thailand, Armenia, Korea, El Salvador, the Philippines, Japan, China, Oaxaca, you name it—but where 85 percent of students are so poor they qualify for free or reduced lunch.

The power of Get Lit Players is not just the poems they've mastered from Walt Whitman, Langston Hughes, and Pablo Neruda, but also their own stories, images, fears, thoughts, visions, and hopes. How they've used singular unique personas and combined them with others to create a dance of words, emotions, and ideas.

These young people, unlike most adults—from politicians to TV personalities to journalists—tread boldly into the hard and nuanced spaces in our society, including the ugly, dark, and forbidden, and bring back a bounty of beauty and truth.

This is transformative the way poetry should be: from the soul of a person to the soul of the world. The impact is deep in one's being but also in our environment, so that the parameters of true justice, equity, cooperation, and freedom are clear and integral yet linked to healing and alignments that make us whole, interconnected, and filled with possibilities that only an engaged imagination and heart can realize.

I'm honored to be part of this book showcasing how the vitality of our youth is still intact despite many economic, political, and cultural barriers. Get Lit Players are for real, in a time when "real" is often deceit, manipulation, and illusion. They prove that there is no greater morality than the morality of living out a full, destined, and adequately resourced life.

Luis J. Rodriguez is Poet Laureate of Los Angeles, author of Always Running: La Vida Loca: Gang Days in LA, *as well as founding editor of Tia Chucha Press and cofounder of Tia Chucha's Cultural Center & Bookstore in the San Fernando Valley.*

INTRODUCTION

In Los Angeles, the Get Lit Players are kind of like rock stars. They perform for thousands of their peers each year, and teens from California to Iceland can recite their work by heart. Kids create fan pages and fan art devoted to them. The Players are famous for the poems they perform by classic poets like Maya Angelou, Jimmy Santiago Baca, Langston Hughes, Pablo Neruda, and so on, and for the poems that they create in response to those classics—like Maia's "Perfect," Raul's "Can I Speak About My Culture?" and Rhiannon's "Smile." These poetic responses are actually studied in schools. In a time when power stems from popularity, these poets are throwing their power to things that matter, with their own words and self-expression as their tools.

What is poetry, you ask? Poetry is a language of the soul. It is the way we express the things that can't be said. It is the truth escaping from our kneecaps and eyes and fingers, bursting out of our pores and our pens. It is THE TRUTH without filter or interference of mind, society, rightfulness, or appropriateness. It is what we feel and never say. It is a melding of all of the feelings we had as children before we tucked those feelings away. It is who we were before our first hurt and who we've become since. It is the voice of our innermost selves, without judgment. It is the friend we never thought we'd have. It is truth before grammar and structure and school. It is also the cultivated stream *after* grammar and structure and school. It is learning to take that wild, natural earthquake inside and shape it, share it— through precision, thought, and skill. It is a means to communicate secrets of the soul with others—a new language, a new way to bring what's wild into the world.

Poetry is everywhere! It is the lines printed on coffee mugs, the chants of the playground, the poignant prayers of childhood, the songs we can't stop singing. I have watched poetry change lives. It has changed mine. Maybe it will change yours too.

Get Lit was founded in 2006, and it now reaches over tens of thousands of young people each year who transform their lives, families, and communities through the art and social activism that comes from finding one's voice. Get Lit builds scholars—not statistics—through this youth-led revolution that lets teens reclaim their educations and unearth their potential. There are students who literally go to school just so they can go to Get Lit. We've seen poets go from impoverished backgrounds to elite universities and beyond.

This is a real revolution, and it is needed now more than ever. Here are the numbers: 98 percent of our Get Lit Players go to college, 70 percent with merit-based scholarships. Over 97 percent of teachers see a significant increase in attendance, engagement, and academic excellence in students who have completed the Get Lit curriculum. Amid California's literacy crisis, Get Lit is a homegrown, award-winning remedy that is now taught all over the globe. Our simple but unique methodology is used in schools by teachers and also by student youth leaders, from Bakersfield to Baton Rouge to Brazil.

The Get Lit Players are the ambassadors of this work, and each year they are selected through an arduous audition process. These are the poets you will meet in this book. They have, over the past few years, burst to international repute by spitting their own raw, fearless truth. They have garnered over one hundred million views on YouTube. The website Upworthy has called them "fearless." *GOOD Magazine* in Iceland titled them "The Teen Spoken Word Poets that Enchanted the Internet." They have performed alongside poets and musicians across the globe, including Questlove at the Kennedy Center in DC, Gloria Steinem on *The Queen Latifah Show*, and John Legend at the Hollywood Bowl. They've even been invited to the White House. In 2014 and 2015, the Get Lit Players performed at the Women in the World Summit at Lincoln Center alongside the likes of Hillary Clinton, Meryl Streep, and Angelina Jolie. They wrote the manifesto for Dove's #ChooseBeautiful campaign as well as the preamble to the 2015 Global Goals of the United Nations. They are teaching Los Angeles, America, and the world that the voices of youth matter. *Your* voice matters. *You* matter.

The young poets who come out of the Get Lit program defy the limits flung at them by society. Why must society label and categorize everything? We are *all* human. In the words of Henry David Thoreau, "All men are children, and of one family. The same tale sends them all to bed, and wakes them in the morning."

Most of us learn this beautiful lesson the hard way. In the movie *Milk*, iconic LGBT activist Harvey Milk (played by Sean Penn) gets a nasty letter with an insulting drawing of himself. Rather than throw it away or stuff it in a drawer, Harvey Milk posts it on his refrigerator. He says we need to look at what people are calling us—stare it straight in the face. Only then will it lose its power. The monster is the scariest when it's under your bed.

Like all of us, the poets you will encounter on these pages have been labeled. When asked for the name we endured the longest or the stereotype that stung the worst, we answered. Labeling is dangerous because it's easy.

Real truth is complicated. It is contradictory. It is ever changing. As we are. In the words of Walt Whitman:

> *Do I contradict myself?*
> *Very well, then I contradict myself.*
> *(I am large. I contain multitudes.)*

The time has come to set ourselves free.
This is a revolution. This is a literary riot.
Read on.

—DIANE LUBY LANE
FOUNDER AND EXECUTIVE DIRECTOR OF
GET LIT—WORDS IGNITE

HOW THIS BOOK WORKS

With this book, you can gain entry into the world of words and start benefiting from the power of poetry.

In each chapter, you will be introduced to a Get Lit poet and their personal story. You will then read the classic poem that most inspired them and the response poem they wrote based on that classic. Then you will be given writing prompts and further reading so you can write poems of your own. You might be asking why. Well, the answer is simple: this technique works. It has produced magic, time and time again. And it can create magic for you.

The Stories

This book features the stories and work of nineteen young poets. In Los Angeles literacy rates are staggeringly low, with dropout rates incredibly high. But these young poets are changing that in their schools and communities. And if it can change in LA, it can change anywhere!

These poets are superheroes whose superpower has been to transform their experiences, their differences, their trials, and their triumphs into alchemical gold through poetry. They come from all walks of life. They are different in so many ways, and yet, on a core level, they are also the same as every other breathing person on this planet. They, like you, have something to say, and they deserve to be heard. They have a story, and their story is important.

So is yours.

Scratch beneath the surface. Ask questions. Go deeper.

Claim your classic.

You will be exposed to the classic poems that have been inspiring people since long before Get Lit started. These masters will give you a direct path to go deep, accessing your soul, your pain, your past, and your future. You will know which poems are for you because they will speak to you. They will make your breath quicken; they will make the hair on the back of your neck stand up; they will make you feel seen and understood like never before. That's when you know a poem is yours. When you find your poem, stay with it for a while. Live with it; read it at different times of the day; memorize it. When you do this, it becomes a part of you, and you become a part of it.

Great art is immortal. It never dies. A classic isn't a classic because it's old; it's a classic because it's *GREAT*. In fact, most of the things artists reach for are impossible to realize in their lifetimes. And great books are sacred texts that can't be reduced to one time and place. Works like *Leaves of Grass*, *Don Quixote*, and *The Autobiography of Malcolm X* come into this world profoundly incomplete; they are waiting for next generations to ask the right questions. Every subsequent generation helps complete them. Our continued listening to the words keeps the thoughts alive, and also keeps us connected to the people who have come before us and the people who will come after us.

Classics are not for an elite few—they are for everyone. These great artists were as human as any of us. Tolstoy was excommunicated by the pope. Emily Dickinson was shy and died with over one thousand unpublished poems in her drawer. Dostoyevsky was a gambler. Their human traits were unique, but what they shared in common was their love for people, and their hunger and their need for existence and expression.

Respond in your own voice.

The classic poems remind us that our experiences are universal, and that means we are never truly alone. Responding to them with your own writing is the heart of Get Lit. Answering back to a poem with your own words, your own poems, is natural—it creates a dialogue. You're having a conversation with great poets! You're having conversations with Walt Whitman, Lucille Clifton, and Tupac Shakur!

UN Ambassador Nancy Rubin once said, "Paper is the best listener in the world." Well, by creating response poems, you can benefit from the wisdom of those you admire and become part of a great lineage of self-expression and courage. When you read each chapter, be a detective: pay attention to the author's personal story; then see which classic poem they chose and how they responded to it with their own personal poetry. Then we'll walk you through it so that you can do it too.

This book will guide you.

The questions at the end of each chapter will help spark your own flames of creativity for those who want to write but don't know how to begin. And for those who are already writing but want some focus, the prompts will fan your flames . . . transporting you to unexplored areas, mining your life and mind for experiences you can use in your writing.

Embrace the wisdom of the masters.

At the end of each chapter is a list of classic poems for further reading. You can access many of these poems for free by googling. You can also check out poem anthologies at your local library. You will be able to find the poets who inspire you most. Maybe it will be Mary Oliver for her love of nature, or Billy Collins for his humor, or Rumi for his ability to inspire faith and hope, or Charles Bukowski for his candor.

Carry the revolution in your community.

Finally, at the end of the book, in addition to writing and performance guidance, you will find information about how to join a poetry group or start one of your own. You'll find out how to stay in touch with us at Get Lit. We want to hear from you and be of use to you on your own path to revolution.

Use this book to discover things about yourself. Let poetry enhance your life and, in turn, improve your community and the world.

Welcome to our family.

EARTHQUAKE
RAUL HERRERA

"Earthquake" has been performed as an individual poem, two-person poem, and even three-person poem. Most commonly performed as a duo poem, it has been performed at colleges and universities and at every kind of political event and commemoration imaginable. It's about the importance of honoring our ancestors and finding our voice.

Person 1: In 1906 an 8.2-sized earthquake ruptured the San
       Andreas Fault, killing an estimated 3,000 people.

2: If vibrations break boulders and devastate lives,

Then our words can split open minds and alter the geo-
       graphical shape of its content.

1: Because sound is vibration.

2: Our verbs are its earthquakes

ALL: And our hands are much like the Richter scale.

1: Charting the magnitude of our words.

2: So when you write,

ALL: Fight the urge to destroy your enemies.

2: Because an earthquake,

1: named Gandhi

2: once told me,

ALL: Even revenge has aftershocks.

2: That even a whisper

ALL: Can cause a revolution.

1: In 2010 a 7.0-sized earthquake takes the lives of 300,000
       Haitians.

2: Do not underestimate

ALL: The Hercules behind your tongue.

2: Your voices are the reasons this planet's axis is tilted.

1: But your silence is the reason this planet is dying.

ALL: So let's cause a ruckus!

2: If Earthquakes can destroy lives,

ALL: Our voices can rebuild them.

1: In 2011 a 9.0-earthquake demolishes Fukushima, Japan.

"I have been to the mountaintop and I looked over and I've
       seen the

Promised land."

2: But the only thing in our way

ALL: Is a mute mountain.

2: So we

ALL: Crumble mountains.

2: We

ALL: Crack rock

2: without needing a pipe.

1: Just give me a word.

2: One sentence can make the ground move like a Tsunami.

ALL: You can see their words cracking the concrete.

1: Cracking

2: Like the backs of the rebels from the past.

1: Cracking

2: Like the blast that killed 2Pac's laugh.

ALL: Malcolm exited this world

2: believing that his earthquake would cause repercussions.

1: "The future belongs to those who prepare for it today."

2: So today I have a dream.

1: But my dream wasn't heard

2: Today I have a dream

1: But my dream was deferred

2: Today I had a dream about a King but the king wasn't heard.

ALL: The legends are angry.

2: The world is violent

ALL: While we stay...
     Why?

2: Newton's 3rd law states,

1: "For every action there is an equal and opposite reaction."

2: For example, if the action is

1: division

2: then the opposite reaction would be

1: communication.

2: Problems react to solutions.

ALL: Oppression reacts to revolution.

The death of Trayvon Martin reacts to Zimmerman's
    prosecution.

2: Now this is law.

2: Voices react to vibrations,

ALL: Vibrations react to earthquakes.

2: So if sound is vibration

ALL: Our verbs are its earthquakes.

2: So let's break the ground our fallen heroes are trapped
    underneath.
    Resurrect poets from graves

ALL: REACT

2: Leaders from being slayed

ALL: REACT

2: Let's speak with tremors trembling towers.

ALL: Talk like an earthquake.
    Be like a rock,

2: And watch this granite planet

ALL: Shake.

1

LOSER

MAIA MAYOR, 17

Maia's Story

Sometimes I think about my past failures and I get sad, no matter how inconsequential they seem to be. That time I forgot the lines to a poem onstage and had to read it from my cell phone. That time when no one clapped. Those other times when no one clapped. That time I poured my heart out and then noticed a student sleeping at her desk. That time I made a collect call out of curiosity and had to pay my friend's mother fifty cents. That time I failed Spanish. That time I failed Korean. That time I failed French. That time I failed ASL.

It is a deep hurt, igniting several other pangs of regret and remorse and embarrassment that come rushing up all at once. And it scares me to know that I am capable of feeling so much all at once. My heart drops into the pit of my stomach when I remember the time I called my mother "ugly." Fifteen years later and I still want to cry. My heart beats faster and my chest feels like it's going to implode. My throat closes up. Every part of my body hurts. I think about the time she got me a present I didn't like and how I left it in the backseat of her car despite her constant reminders. I find it hard to breathe. I can feel it up in my throat and squirming in my bottom jaw. My stomach hurts. I am dizzy. But I wrap my arms around my chest and suppress anything trying to jump out.

When my grandma talks about wanting to die, when she confronts me with the brutal reality of the inevitable, I don't react. I am unaffected. I am buttering my toast. I am detached because it's the only way to keep my spine straight and my feet on the floor. I will not want to go to her funeral. I will not want to visit her grave. I will want to stay as far away as possible. Nothing in this world scares me more than the fragility of human life.

I expel pain at insignificant moments. To the dog shelter commercial, you may have my tears. You may have my quivering lip and wobbling shoulders. You may have my broken heart, my sobbing, my short gasps of breath. Because I do not want to cry in my grandma's absence. Because I am afraid of what will pour out of me. I am afraid of running out of tears and out of breath and out of feeling. I am afraid of being empty. I don't think my body will be able to handle it. I don't know how I'll find the strength to open my eyes and rise to my feet every morning.

I imagine this to be a concentrated version of my entire life. First I feel lost. And then I feel angry and upset with myself and with the world. And every bad thought and feeling that has ever passed through me comes crashing down all at once. And it progressively gets harder to breathe. I have a climactic existential crisis before eventually giving up. I briefly feel relieved. And then nothing at all. And I settle into a comfortable numbness.

At my best, I am dramatic, self-serving, and ruthless. At my worst, I am vacant and underwhelming. The spectrum of my personality is built like a looping roller coaster where everyone, including myself, tends to feel a little nauseated. I am crippled by anxiety and depression; I have been all my life. And I have learned to suffer quietly, letting opportunities pass me by on every occasion because I don't feel capable. This is how I live my life . . . with everything just out of arm's reach. This is why I've been kicked out of school seven times. This is why I still can't drive. This is why my group of friends could be counted on an amputated hand. This is why my answer will always be no. I am perpetually on the cusp of greatness. But emotional instability and a deep-rooted fear of failure keep me tiptoeing through life like every task is an intricate puzzle made of broken glass. To be perfectly honest, I am the most terrified person you will ever meet. I am afraid of vulnerability, of inadequacy, of embarrassment, of imperfection, of death. Of life, for that matter. But I'm figuring it out one step at a time.

My first attempt at facing my fears started at the hands of my mother, whose love of language inspired me to express myself in ways I'd never imagined. My mother is Japanese, and when I was little, she used to teach me words and phrases, but one I still think of often is *kintsukuroi*, meaning "to repair with gold." It's the art of repairing pottery with gold or silver lacquer and understanding that the piece is more beautiful for having been broken. That is essentially what the Leonard Cohen poem (in the form of song lyrics) from "Anthem" means to me.

My response poem, "Perfect," came from a dark place. From desperation and uncontrollable rage. And while I may *never* bloom into a self-assured optimist, the experience of connecting to Cohen's words, responding with my own, and performing them live was transformative to say the least. (And far more cathartic than the empty promises of Prozac.) I spent years striving for unattainable ideas of perfection, but I view this poem as a profoundly important reminder that perfection is beside the point. We are all inherently flawed. There will always be a crack in everything. But that is where you find the light. That is where the raw honesty and the beauty of vulnerability lie.

Classic Poem

From "Anthem" by Leonard Cohen
Ring the bells that still can ring
Forget your perfect offering
There is a crack in everything
That's how the light gets in.

Response Poem

Perfect
Maia Mayor

Is there something wrong with you,
a loose screw or two that ruined your ability to function?
Why are you always so tired?
Your life is uninspired and small; all you do is sprawl on the
    couch
with outstretched limbs like a sloth in slow motion.
Where is your devotion to succeed, Maia?
Did it drift out your window with the smoke from your weed?
Do I need to force-feed you discipline 'til you finally
    concede?
I cook and I clean and I don't stop 'til the soles of my feet
    bleed.
But I'm fine.
I'm perfect.
Be perfect, Maia.
Be perfect like me.

Stop wearing those god-awful ripped pants
and that lipstick like a whore with Double-D implants.

You only get one chance.
Stop acting like a cat with nine lives left.
Stop committing yourself to songs and stories and spoken
    slam bullshit
in a world where degrees and PhDs impede the need for
    poetry.
And stop chewing on your nails.
No wonder you've never attracted any males.
Why do you do that? Do you like the taste? Are they
    sweet?
You can't eat sweets, Maia.
You're ruining your teeth like you're ruining your life.
My teeth are perfect. Clean and pristine.
They gleam like the golden halo above my perfectly con-
    ditioned head.
I don't need sugar, Maia.
I am above sugar.

Why are you down here, Maia?
Why are you down here when you need to be up here?
Up here with the ones who have a promising career
who listen when information goes in one ear
and doesn't come out the other.
You'll never be up here, Maia.
You act as if the act of listening is a crime
or you would have heard me the six hundred and sixty-
    sixth time
I told you to STOP CHEWING ON YOUR NAILS.
Stop chewing on your nails like a goddamn piece of trash.
You can't be trash, Maia.
You have to be perfect.
Be perfect like me.

I get up at 5 in the morning every day.

I start my day the same way worried that I'll collapse

as my bones start to decay from cleaning up your scraps.

Why is your room such a mess?

The clothes go in the hamper, Maia.

Not displayed on your bed like your lack of morals.

Not littered on the floor collecting more dust than my with-
     ered expectations.

You disregard my rules with stubborn contempt

in a substandard attempt at teenage rebellion.

But you can't be a rebel, Maia.

You're not interesting enough.

You need to obey and say "Yes" and "Okay,"

you need to do it with a smile on your less-than-average
     face.

You need to try harder, Maia.

Make it wider, Maia.

Why don't you know how to smile?

You disappoint me, Maia.

You never appreciate what I do for you.

You never try to be a winner.

And you never eat your dinner.

You never eat the dinner I consistently provide for you

as I constantly remind you of the life I set aside for you.

That meal doesn't pay for itself.

I don't care if it's ideal, stop telling me how you feel.

You need to eat it.

Eat it all.

Eat it at a reasonable time with a glass of milk.

You need milk, Maia.

You need calcium like you need a catalyst for growth.

You'll never grow to be tall.
Be tall like me.
I drink my milk, Maia.
Drink your fucking milk.
Be tall.
Be perfect.
Be perfect like me.

You need to pay more attention, Maia.
Stop daydreaming, Maia.
Stop staring at the ceiling as if your one redeeming quality
    lies hidden in the plaster.
You need to organize your life.
Your life is a disaster
just like your room.
Just like your teeth.
Just like your future,
which will soon come to an end if you don't put down that
    pen.
You need to stop writing, Maia.
Your life is not a book.
Don't give me that look, Maia.
I'm just trying to help you.
I'm just trying to love you.
I'm just trying to love you.
You have to let me love you
so that you can be perfect.
Be perfect like me.

Get Writing

Look in.

1. Have you ever felt like a loser? When?
2. How do you deal with your failures and mistakes?
3. Tell the story of a time you failed and picked yourself up.
4. Do you sabotage yourself by not finishing what you started or by not trying your best?

SHOUT out.

1. Pick a line, a word, a phrase, or an image from Maia's poem "Perfect" that made you feel understood or made you feel worse about yourself. Talk back to it. Yell. Convince. Set your timer for ten minutes and keep your hand moving. Write a poem using that line, word, phrase, or image that inspired you.
2. Write about something you haven't finished and how finishing it might change your life.

Claim your classic.

Classic Poems on Feeling Deeply and Getting Out of Your Own Way

"A Black Sky Hates the Moon," Rumi

"Agonies are one of my changes of garments . . ." from "Song of Myself," *Leaves of Grass*, Walt Whitman

"Bluebird," Charles Bukowski

"Lost," David Wagoner

"Saturday at the Canal," Gary Soto

"Stone," Charles Simic

"The Breeze at Dawn," Rumi
"The Obligation to Be Happy," Linda Pastan
"Truth," Gwendolyn Brooks
"Yellow Glove," Naomi Shihab Nye

> You must have chaos within you to give birth to a dancing star.
> —**Friedrich Nietzsche**

GRINGO

RAUL HERRERA, 19

Raul's Story

The story about to be told is not to evoke sympathy or to inspire but to inform those who believe sorrow and struggle cannot be transformed into art. We all hold a struggle within us that either stands as a motivator or a tormentor. If I had stood in my room sulking about my life, I would have never discovered the beauty *within me.*

I believe that if I had never overcome my particular hardships, I would not be the person I am today. I allow myself to be sensitive because my father taught me how not to be. I allow myself to talk about how I feel because my father taught me how not to. I believe that the best artists are products of the worst circumstances, not because of the trouble their lives contain but because they alter that trouble into a lesson—an example for those in similar situations.

When I was twelve, an unforeseen tragedy struck home. Eventually the money ran out and the bills accumulated into an insurmountable amount. We pawned the cars and lost the house to the bank, leaving us living in a two-bedroom apartment with eight other people for a year. Trying to pay attention to literary devices and MLA format in my English honors class while thinking about the misery that waited at home was no easy task.

School was tough, but I got through it by writing down how I felt about what I was going through. I then helped create a poetry club at my high school to allow fellow students the opportunity to express and share their own struggles and stories. If I had never let my emotions out—let my story out—I would never have reached out to others to help them do that very same thing. It is such a therapeutic action to write your woes onto paper. By bringing your fears and sadness into the physical world, you allow yourself to transform those emotions into reasons to be brave, reasons to be fearless. Once I became comfortable with who I was, I was able to voice my thoughts and identity with pride. Where I came from was suddenly a place I was proud of. My appearance was no longer an apology but a statement. Writing—more specifically, writing poetry—served as an opportunity for me to realize that our social, cultural, and financial history are all positive contributors to how we identify with the world.

Once poetry had its grip on me, my culture was a subject I wanted to know everything about. Shortly after, I was introduced to Michelle Serros's poem. It reminded me that cultural identity is an ongoing process. Cultural background can be a significant tool for helping one become self-aware, but it can also be a label that is used to limit or judge an individual or group. This poem made me think about remembering where we come from. Without fear of prejudice or criticism, I attempted to express not only the struggle of mastering my native tongue but also the struggle attached to being a Mexican American in present-day America. The connection between the classic poem and my response is the desire to reclaim my culture.

Classic Poem

Mi Problema
Michele Serros
My sincerity isn't good enough.
Eyebrows raise
when I request:

"Hable mas despacio, por favor."
My skin is brown
just like theirs,
but now I'm unworthy of the color
'cause I don't speak Spanish
the way I should.
Then they laugh and talk about
mi problema
in the language I stumble over.

A white person gets encouragement,
praise,
for weak attempts at a second language.
"Maybe he wants to be brown
like us."
and that is good.

My earnest attempts
make me look bad,
dumb.

"Perhaps she wanted to be white
like THEM."
and that is bad.

I keep my flash cards hidden
a practice cassette tape
not labeled
'cause I am ashamed.
I "should know better"
they tell me
Spanish is in your blood.

I search for SSL classes,
(Spanish as a Second Language)
in college catalogs
and practice
with my grandma,
who gives me patience,
permission to learn.

And then one day,
I'll be a perfected "r" rolling
tilde using Spanish speaker.
A true Mexican at last!

Response Poem

Can I Speak About My Culture?
Raul Herrera

Can I speak about my culture?
Can I...I...I
I speak Spanish but I don't have an accent
I am full-blooded Mexicano so cholo is the motto
If anyone is asking
I...I...I have a schizophrenic tongue

Escucha me mientras yo digo mas verdad que los libros
    historicos Americanos
Hear me while I speak more truth than American history
    books
American history crooks. They are panicking. He is panick-
    ing. Hispanic.
Tell 'em politicians how you took California
Tell 'em politicians how you took Arizona
I...I...I urge you, Arizona, not to bring prejudice to the peo-
    ple who used to call that land home
Para la tierra usted robó es la tierra que ellos poseyeron
For the land you stole is the land they owned
I am finally learning to speak Spanish just for this poem
Because how are you supposed to move your people if you
    don't speak their language?
Can I speak about my culture?
Can I...I...I say that the culture of all humanity is unity.
So why segregate when we're in this together?
Why alienate when it's a human endeavor?
Society is full of alienations; try to kick them out so back
    to your spaceships.
Back to being racist and back to the basics.
The truth is right in front of us then why don't we
    face it?
Beauty, wealth, power, and color. It's all overrated.
I...I...Isolated and I...I so Latin and I...I'm so hated
The box that we're trapped in divides us in fractions
Take out your tongues and let's speak some action
Mi lengua es un pulmón que no ha ampliado todavía
My tongue is a lung that hasn't expanded yet
But if I continue to eat my culture, I will never run out of
    breath

We have brown skin resembling the dirt roads we've been
traveling looking for freedom

But only found a freeway.

At the end of freeways we sell dreams in crates while the
fruits of our labors are ravaged by greedy mouths.

I'm just waiting for the day they bite down on their tongues
and spit out the truth.

Can I speak about my culture?

Can I...I...I don't consider Mexicans to be special but I do
consider us equal

So when you start attacking my people through the definition of legal

Expect a few angry Latinos. ok

I...I...I am tired of being discriminated against. But
aren't we all?

So tell me I should get over it.

Like the border, like the Dream Act, like anti-immigration
laws.

That's like telling Asians to get over the exploitation of
opium to build the railroads.

That's like telling African Americans to get over slavery

Or Native Americans to get over America

Por lo que no tenga miedo de recordar

So don't be afraid to remember.

Recuerde su cultura

Remember your culture.

Before it forgets you.

Can I speak about my culture?

Can I...I...I speak.

Get Writing

Look in.

1. How have you transformed "sorrow and struggle" into art?
2. What woes do you have that are waiting to be expressed creatively?
3. How have you turned your worst experiences into your strongest traits?
4. Whose behavior do you hate, and how have you learned to be unlike that person?
5. How do you wish you could be braver?

SHOUT out.

1. Write a poem about learning to speak the language of someone who doesn't understand you.
2. Write about how your culture informs your identity.

Claim your classic.

Classic Poems for Celebrating One's Heritage and Gaining Meaning from Cultural Identity

"Bilingual/Bilingüe," Rhina Espaillat

"Home," Warsan Shire

"Freshman Class Schedule," Jose Antonio Rodriguez

"Love Rejected," Lucille Clifton

"On the Amtrak from Boston to New York City," Sherman Alexie

"Remember," Joy Harjo

"Speaking With Hands," Luis J. Rodriguez

"Sunrise," Mary Oliver

"The Melting Pot," Dudley Randall

"Who Understands Me but Me," Jimmy Santiago Baca

THUG

WALTER FiNNIE JR., 18

Walter's Story

I've always wondered what life would be like if I were a bird. How would it feel to just spread my wings and fly away from all the troubles I come across in my life? Leave them grounded while I soar as an eagle over every worry, responsibility, distraction, and obstacle I may come across? I've always thought that this would be better, but just recently I started to think otherwise.

My name is Walter Ray Finnie Jr., and I was born to an ex-gang member and an addict. Both my parents are now trying to recover from the past mistakes they made when I was younger. Then you have me, the Dreamer, the one who has always seen the best in every situation.

It's like I was cut from a different cloth because I always had big plans to make a drastic change from the self-destructive path of my family. My father was in and out of jail the majority of my childhood, so my elementary years were spent with my mom. This was before my mother met her life-changing addiction. My life consisted of my daily observations of the weed smoke around me, nodding my head to the sounds of the loud gangster music, and traveling back and forth between my mother's house during the week, for school, and my grandma's house in Watts during the weekend and vacations.

But when I stayed with my grandparents, they kept me busy gardening, landscaping, painting, cutting grass, toying with mechanics, and doing carpentry work. My grandparents always let me know one thing: whatever you do, do your best. So whatever I did, I did it with passion and perfection. I always made the best grades throughout those years, setting a good example for my younger siblings.

By the fifth grade, I had nine siblings: four younger ones from my mom and a mixture—older and younger—of five from my dad. But we are all family.

Fifth grade was a crazy year for me. I was suspended for the first time for fighting, and that's when things started going downhill. The day of my fifth-grade graduation was the last time my little brother Tyrie and I saw our mom, our little sister Kamya, and our brother Jahmale for a long time. We moved in with my grandparents.

My grandparents shaped my life because they taught me how to love a family, care for others, and give back and appreciate. But Granny (who was in charge, even over Grandpa) had a big load on her plate. She had custody of me and Tyrie, plus she adopted all seven of my father's children (his and my stepmother's) because he went back to jail. Granny also had children of her own, some of whom still lived at home. We all lived together in one four-bedroom house. It was packed.

Life was hard, but my Granny made it work. She pushed me through middle school and kept me in church, which I needed because middle school was no piece of cake. I was angry at my mother, who was who knows where, and at my father, who had just gotten out of jail. I had a short temper, which led to unnecessary fights and suspensions. Kids tried to bully me too. Back then, I felt like I had a point to prove, just because I didn't always have all the new stuff like other kids.

By eighth grade, I started to grow up a bit. I knew I couldn't give up on my younger siblings, so I got on the ball. Then, second semester, my mom started to show her face again. I was mowing the front yard when she rolled up in a black Pontiac. When I looked at her, my eyes filled with tears that never fell. Her face was really skinny and her eyes were swollen. I had never seen her like that, and it scared me. But she kissed me on the cheek, got back in that black car, and said, "I love you." I stood there and watched her leave, then continued to cut the grass.

Before all this mess, I would always tell my mom I was gonna build her a house someday. I wanted to be an architect. And that's all I could think about after watching those brake lights disappear. Someday I would get her a place to live. I felt sad and angry. I was determined to make our lives better someday.

A couple of weeks later, Mama came back pregnant, looking like she was ready to drop any minute. I hadn't seen her for some time, only as she passed me by on the street, speaking to me from the inside of cars. Now I couldn't wait to graduate because this new baby had forced my mother to sober up, and I would be able to spend the summer with her. She was staying in a facility for single mothers who were recovering from addiction, and the place offered therapy for children of addicts as well.

I graduated from eighth grade and went to stay with my mom in the program for the summer. But things soon took a devastating turn. My new baby brother died from SIDS (sudden infant death syndrome), and I was scared that my mom would relapse. It hit her hard, but she stayed strong and didn't break. She kept her sobriety. Afterward, I felt like my mom needed her children, so my brother and I went back to living with her in Compton. Back to the ghetto, back to the place I was supposed to get away from—the place that would clip my wings. But I didn't care. I was back with Mama.

When I was in eleventh grade we moved with my mother back to Watts, the hometown of my father's gang and a place that eats the good alive. This is when life started to take some drastic turns, for better and for worse. It's when I realized that dreaming about being a bird wouldn't help my situation; it would only make it worse.

My mother had custody of all her children once again. My younger siblings' dad moved in with us, and for the first year, we were living well. The apartment was all plushed out, and we had everything we needed. So for me, it was go to school and smoke the best weed daily, because it was all around me.

This took its toll on everybody. The weed made me lazy: I barely kept up with my studies and I completely stopped doing chores. One of the big things that got under my mother's skin back then was a dirty apartment, and that's what she came home to every day: a dirty place that reeked of ganja. Hard for a recovering addict. But I didn't notice because I was so distracted by the people and happenings around me.

It wasn't until the day my mother finally lost it that I started to see what was really going on. I found out my stepdad was cheating on her and she relapsed after six years of being sober. And once my mom relapsed, my stepdad shook with his new chick and didn't even look back at his kids. My pops was in jail and my mom was long gone, so it was up to me to keep us in our house. I left school and held it down. I had to get on the block; I had to slang; I had to do so many things that I was uncomfortable with. But when I came home and saw the pain and hunger in my sisters' eyes, I was enraged. I had to make it better for them.

I kept the apartment and family intact for as long as I could, but after three months, the people were onto me. The manager of the apartment complex noticed my mother wasn't coming home, and the school counselor called Family Services. Our family got broken up, and we went our separate ways for a while. I bounced around here and there until I moved in with an old friend. His family gave me and my brother Tyrie a home.

I finally had a chance to go back to school, and that's when I met poetry. I have always loved writing raps, but when I got into this class called Get Lit, my life changed. At first, Get Lit was held after school. I was expelled from school for truancy, so I didn't know about it. When I came back to the school one day to visit, I was surprised to hear kids upstairs performing poetry. I wanted to do it too. So I got back into school and had to stay in classes all day just to get to that poetry class after school.

Next thing you know, I tried out for my school's Classic Slam team and made it. This meant I'd be representing our school by competing in this citywide poetry competition called the Classic Slam. Thousands of kids compete there, and it was my first time really performing onstage. I performed Langston Hughes's "The Negro Mother" and my response, "Negro Brother," and "A Poem For Third World Brothers" by Etheridge Knight as a group poem, along with our group response called "White America." My team and I got our asses kicked, but Diane noticed me and Kyland Turner (featured later in this book) and asked us to audition to be Get Lit Players. We made it, and that year was one of the best years of my life. I went from nothing to performing at Dodger Stadium for more than fifteen thousand kids in Los Angeles, to flying all over the country, and eventually, to getting a scholarship to attend Lincoln University in Pennsylvania, which was Langston Hughes's alma mater.

Now I don't wonder what it would be like to be a bird because I'm already a bird. My words are my wings and they make me fly over everything that may get in my path.

Classic Poem

The Negro Mother
Langston Hughes

Children, I come back today
To tell you a story of the long dark way
That I had to climb, that I had to know
In order that the race might live and grow.
Look at my face—dark as the night—
Yet shining like the sun with love's true light.
I am the dark girl who crossed the red sea
Carrying in my body the seed of the free.
I am the woman who worked in the field
Bringing the cotton and the corn to yield.
I am the one who labored as a slave,
Beaten and mistreated for the work that I gave—
Children sold away from me, husband sold, too.
No safety, no love, no respect was I due.
Three hundred years in the deepest South:
But God put a song and a prayer in my mouth.
God put a dream like steel in my soul.
Now, through my children, I'm reaching the goal.
Now, through my children, young and free,
I realized the blessing denied to me.
I couldn't read then. I couldn't write.
I had nothing, back there in the night.
Sometimes, the valley was filled with tears,
But I kept trudging on through the lonely years.
Sometimes, the road was hot with the sun,
But I had to keep on till my work was done:
I had to keep on! No stopping for me—
I was the seed of the coming Free.

I nourished the dream that nothing could smother
Deep in my breast—the Negro mother.
I had only hope then, but now through you,
Dark ones of today, my dreams must come true:
All you dark children in the world out there,
Remember my sweat, my pain, my despair.
Remember my years, heavy with sorrow—
And make of those years a torch for tomorrow.
Make of my pass a road to the light
Out of the darkness, the ignorance, the night.
Lift high my banner out of the dust.
Stand like free men supporting my trust.
Believe in the right, let none push you back.
Remember the whip and the slaver's track.
Remember how the strong in struggle and strife
Still bar you the way, and deny you life—
But march ever forward, breaking down bars.
Look ever upward at the sun and the stars.
Oh, my dark children, may my dreams and my prayers
Impel you forever up the great stairs—
For I will be with you till no white brother
Dares keep down the children of the Negro Mother.

Response Poem

The Negro Brother
Walter Finnie Jr.

My fellow sisters and my brothers,
I must tell you of Mother.
She won't be coming home, so listen to your brother:
we have a major situation on hand,

but for me it's not my first time.
Just imagine seeing different men
in and out through the night,
I used to look with such fire in my eyes
so many tears to cry,
and not enough strength to try
and stop the fools.
Had my mind swimming like pools,
but as a young dude it really wasn't nothing
that I could do but as I grew up and seen
the different things, I piece together the scene
so I can make it out of the bad dream
that I call my life.
Children, I have sacrificed my life to better yours.
While I try to keep you jovial,
I'm praying she don't overdose
I'm dealing with these overflows
and wearing the same clothes,
it's such a shame, bro, but it's not a game, bro.
But it's very stressful,
that's why I let these words flow
like a river or a Pac verse
I've seen the worst, I put my baby brother in a hearse
and it hurts.
But I don't give up, and that's because I live up
to my own expectations, dreams, memories, and goals
gotta know the separation.
And it's ironic that this drug has my mom and I have you kids,
but now I have to sell this drug just to pay the bills.
But now it's time for school, so have a good day, kids.
Now I'm calling my mother...

Hello, Mother, it's me, your firstborn.
You named me Walter after my dad,
do you remember me, Mother?
Well I'm glad you didn't answer
cuz I got so much to say so,
when you come to, just put it on replay.
Look, I've been taking days off
my feelings got me way out
I wish for a better life,
but I just watch this play out
a way out I'm trying to find it and it's destined
to me, I put my heart into this verse
as it caresses the piece, I'm sleep
my dreams is like my life just pressing repeat,
don't sleep much so when I sleep
I'm having scarier dreams I seen
my mom's on the corner.
With them arrogant fiends
the car pulled up, bussed 3 shots
the end of that dream, I screamed.
Busting out sweats, I get to wiping my neck
and then I pray that she's okay, then I'll just light me a
        spliff...
I trip and then I let go. Like it's the end of that road,
I know, so cold, but still, man, I could never lose hope.
But I'm tired of the problems from you,
and it only hurts cuz you're my mom
and you know that I love you
nothing gets put up above you,
not even my education
and important as that is,

damn it's devastating,

but this is how you repay me?

Ma, that's scandalous,

I've been shot at, jacked, jumped, stabbed,

and just damaged, just to get you back at the house.

I even ran from the police with some crack in my mouth

just for you.

It's been months since I've seen you and the kids, too,

you left us all heartbroken that's what you did do.

Now I'm babysitting your kids, you see the colors of our skin?

You just another statistic, but me...

I'm different

got the strength of 10 men

and though this life is intense, I guarantee we resist it

I'm talking about your sickness, because your

heartless decisions have affected your children

while I'm pushing them toward success

so their lifestyles would be different.

You been missing so much it's to the point we really ain't

tripping,

so on my end,

not one damn f-u-c-k

will be given.

Get Writing

Look in.

1. Tell the story of a time you felt you couldn't face the reality of your
   life.

2. Talk about a time when you felt totally overwhelmed.

3. Write about when you felt people judged you by your outside appearance without knowing anything about your insides.

4. Is there some part of your life you're trying to escape or fly away from? Which part?

SHOUT out.

1. Walter wrote, "I've always wondered what life would be like if I were a bird. How would it feel to just spread my wings and fly away from all the troubles I come across in my life?" Find your own metaphor for how you'd like to deal with the troubles in your life, and use that metaphor to write about them.

2. Find some metaphors from other poems that speak to you. Write them on the top of a page and expand on each of them.

Claim your classic.

Classic Poems on Race, Urban Poverty, Family, and the Life Force

"Ancestors," Dudley Randall

"Dark August," Derek Walcott

"Destiny," Haki Madhubuti

"Do not go gentle into that good night," Dylan Thomas

"Dropping Keys," Hafiz

"Small Prayer for Falling Angels," Lenore Kandel

"Speech to the Young: Speech to the Progress-Toward," Gwendolyn Brooks

"Twice the First Time," Saul Williams

"Mortal Man" first excerpt, Kendrick Lamar

4 GEEK
RHIANNON MCGAVIN, 15

Rhiannon's Story

I was born in the middle of a rainstorm. The human body's cells are completely replaced by the end of seven years, so I've technically been through two bodies already. Skin cells on your hands replace faster since you use them so often, so I must've been through thousands by now. I paint and write and garden. I don't mind writing by hand, but I honestly prefer typing; it distances you from what you're saying. When you use a pen, you have to feel yourself shape the words.

I grew up primarily with my mom, but sometimes I'd venture north into fog to visit my father and his new family. When I was seven, I started studying and performing Shakespeare. Shakespeare means a lot to me. So much of that pain and happiness is still relevant today. Like, there's a

Romeo and Juliet playing out somewhere in a war-torn country right now, probably. I hope they end up okay.

I kept good grades while balancing the Bard, poetry, and taking extra classes over the summer for fun. And of course, simple pleasures like gardening, baking, watercolor painting, and amateur botany experiments. In fifth grade, I tried to test whether applying chlorophyll or sugar to bean sprouts would make them grow better. (See, chlorophyll helps the plant process materials into energy, whereas sugar is the final energetic product.) I'm doing the experiment again right now. I can see the pots from where I'm typing this. I guess I'm also trying to figure out if I should motivate myself with things that help me achieve what I'm doing right now or if I should just focus on that sweet, final goal.

In sixth grade, I started making YouTube videos on my channel, the GeekyBlonde. After four years, I have almost 250,000 total views with over 150 videos. In tenth grade, right now, I have a 4.1 GPA while maintaining a semi-healthy sleep cycle and nurturing my strawberry plants.

In my freshmen year of high school, the Get Lit program came to my school! I'd heard about the organization from older students, as well as from knowing the founder's son from our childhood Shakespeare performances with the LA Drama Club, and I was really excited to go to the classes myself. My school's Classic Slam team placed second citywide, and I was the highest scoring individual poet that year with my response to the classic I'd picked, "A Smile to Remember." I chose this as my classic poem because I knew it was a heavy poem, a hard poem, and I wanted to ensure someone with the actual life experience claimed the piece. The tension and fear inspired me most, especially since I'd started taking public transportation to and from school that year; I was learning how to be watchful. The real inspiration actually came from a male gym teacher who saw me in the hallway right before I went home with the stomach flu and told me to smile, even as I was green with nausea.

I believe that there are three kinds of writing and they all tie into each other, so one can't be good at one without acing the others too. To make nonfiction interesting, you need a little poetry and prose about your topic. Since I base so many of my poems off scientific concepts, it definitely requires nonfiction. And prose, which is really my big goal, needs nonfiction as the base and poetry dashed in for a really good read. It'd be cool to write love poems someday, but for now, I'm very happy just being focused on my own growth.

I like to feel things growing. I try to tend to my garden every day. I also try to keep my nails manicured, but the paint usually degrades after a few minutes of sticking my fingers into new dirt. Dirt's great. Plants thrive best when there are lots of nutrients in the soil, and those vitamins come from decaying material. Blooming off dead stuff is kinda my goal in life.

Classic Poem

A Smile to Remember
Charles Bukowski

we had goldfish and they circled around and around
in the bowl on the table near the heavy drapes
covering the picture window and
my mother, always smiling, wanting us all
to be happy, told me, "be happy Henry!"
and she was right: it's better to be happy if you
can
but my father continued to beat her and me several times a week while
raging inside his 6-foot-two frame because he couldn't
understand what was attacking him from within.

my mother, poor fish,
wanting to be happy, beaten two or three times a
week, telling me to be happy: "Henry, smile!
why don't you ever smile?"

and then she would smile, to show me how, and it was the
saddest smile I ever saw
one day the goldfish died, all five of them,
they floated on the water, on their sides, their
eyes still open,
and when my father got home he threw them to the cat
there on the kitchen floor and we watched as my mother
smiled

Response Poem

Smile
Rhiannon McGavin

People don't give girls enough credit.
I'm in 9th grade now,
And the last time I studied a uniquely female narrative in
    English class was 6th grade.
That might not seem like a lot,
Three years,
But it is.
Difference between 12 and 15,
Between girl and...
We're reading *To Kill a Mockingbird* now, and
I was walking home one day,
Thinking about how Dill's hair was described as "duck fluff"
Or how Scout viewed reading as breathing
Or what I'd help my mom make for dinner when—
I guess I was frowning a little, deep in thought—
Someone, a man, a grown man, told me to "smile, sweetheart!"
Odd, isn't it?
Telling some stranger to at least LOOK happy.
You know, it only takes one more muscle than smiling
To punch someone in the teeth.
Blood's better than tears anyway.
Action over thought,
Thoughts left lingering,
Wriggling through veins and vital organs
The cudgel which has bludgeoned countless before,
Because if there's no struggle,
You lose the cold and broken hallelujah of

"Well, at least you fought."
Don't tell sad girls to smile.
Don't tell sad girls to smile,
Because they might be the type who get cut by
Hip bones.
Don't tell sad girls to smile,
Because she might still be trying to scrub
Someone else's sin from her skin.
Hot water, holy water,
It all flows under the same bridge eventually,
And the dead can only feel cold,
So if she can feel the burning water then maybe,
Maybe—
Don't tell sad girls to smile,
Because by allowing herself to feel happy,
She accepts that she knows the contrast too well
And if she does want to smile,
Then she does it for herself,
Or someone she can be vulnerable with,
Not some slack-jawed, hem-hawing, fish-eyed patriarchal
      nice guy
Who doesn't find a frown appealing.
She might have a good goddamn reason to be sad
So don't you tell me to smile.
It is not your mouth.
It is not yours to consume, to kiss,
To find comfort in when the windows rattle in a storm
Or your heart rattles in your rib cage like seeds in the dry
      earth,
Unable to grow without a little water and sunshine and
      tenderness

And if you really want a sad girl to smile,

Then you hold her,

Until you're drenched in perfume

From the gardens you planted in her heart

So that every time her wounds reopen, she bleeds
    bouquets.

But I am not yours to hold.

And if you keep walking around telling sad girls to smile,

No one will want to be.

And if you come any closer,

I'll bite you.

And smile

Red.

Get Writing

Look in.

1. If your body recycles its cells every seven years, which emotional parts would you like to leave behind and which parts would you like to get renewed?

2. When do you feel most empowered?

3. Who is the woman who's most influenced your life?

4. What do you want to change about the world?

5. Have you ever had someone tell you to feel a certain way or act a certain way that didn't match your true feelings? Why do you think they did that? Did you listen to them?

SHOUT out.

1. Find a line in "Smile" that stirs something in you, and write about what that line evokes.
2. Write about the dark feelings you have, specifically the ones people try to talk you out of. Is one of them rage? Sadness? Ambivalence?
3. Write a poem about the emotion that makes you most uncomfortable. Include what you might need to conquer your discomfort.

Claim your classic.

Classic Poems for Feeling Empowered, Amplifying Women's Voices, Social Change, and Helping Things Grow

"Be Nobody's Darling," Alice Walker

"Coping," Audre Lorde

"Fury," Yevgeny Yevtushenko

"Hanging Fire," Audre Lorde

"Miss Rosie," Lucille Clifton

"Rape Poem," Marge Piercy

"Shrinking Women," Lily Myers

"Variation on the Word Sleep," Margaret Atwood

"Hello, the Roses," Mei-mei Berssenbrugge

"Why I Wake Early," Mary Oliver

ORDINARY

HANNAH DAINS, 16

Hannah's Story

I can't tell you the story of the first poem I wrote because I don't remember it myself. There was no lightbulb moment for me—no sudden "Eureka! I can write poetry!" after years of searching for something to occupy my time. On the days when I actually clean my room, I'll sometimes run into old poems—scribbled on dirty paper in my fourth-grade handwriting, filled with attempts at clever rhyme schemes that never really got me anywhere. My first poem ever is a mystery that cannot be solved, but I can tell you the story of my first *good* poem. It's a poem about space, and even though I wrote it over a year ago, I could recite it from memory if you asked. I wrote it for my best friend (at the time), who was depressed and cutting. If I have had any eureka moment, it was that one—the moment I pulled out my phone and started typing and didn't stop until I had written a real, actual slam poem that I wanted to read in front of anyone who would listen.

It took me a while to find an audience. I didn't know that there were any opportunities for people my age to perform poetry until one of my English teachers, Dr. Miller, asked the Get Lit Players to perform. For the first time, I was watching people my age recite their own poetry, and I was watching people I knew react positively to that poetry. Who would have guessed the star player of the basketball team was a poetry nerd just like the rest of us?

After the Get Lit Players performed, Dr. Miller announced that there would soon be auditions for something called the Classic Slam. I scrambled to the front of the auditorium to put down my name as one of those interested in trying out. When I learned that I had to write a response piece to a classic poem for the event, I was disheartened for a moment. (*You mean this isn't the time for me to share my space poem?*) But I finally found something to write about: female empowerment, a topic very near to my heart. I auditioned for my school's slam-poetry team with a response to D. H. Lawrence's "Women Want Fighters for Their Lovers." It was my first time reading a poem aloud, and I hardly believed it was good enough to get me on the team. Imagine my surprise when I was chosen (along with some of my good friends) to represent my school at the Classic Slam! Imagine my surprise when my poem scored nines and tens at the slam itself, or when the founder of Get Lit, Diane Luby Lane, told me that she loved my poem and wanted me to audition for the Get Lit Players!

Suddenly, poetry wasn't something hidden in the Notes app on my phone. It was something I could share, something I was good at. I even found a place to perform my space poem. Turns out I had been living blocks away from a weekly open mic and never even noticed.

When auditions for the Get Lit Players came around, for once, I could see myself being really, truly successful with something. When I got the call telling me I was on the team, I remember running across the quad of my school to tell Dr. Miller, then running all the way back across to tell my friends.

Now that I've been part of the Get Lit Players for a while, I've learned a lot about poetry. Poetry, like any other skill, takes practice, practice, practice. Lucky for me, I've been practicing poetry almost my entire life. Many people, including my fellow poets, are shocked when they find out that I write a new poem every week. But I've been writing for so long that this seems like the natural thing to do. I've been told that to really be good at something, you have to put in ten thousand hours of practice. I'm not about to do any math, but I think I'm well on my way to reaching that number.

One of the most important things about being a poet is the fact that you simply have to write. Even without any inspiration at all, taking the time to scribble down half a sentence a day is enough. I have piles of poems that are too rough to ever see the light of day, but in every haystack of bad poetry, there's a silver needle somewhere. (I know the haystack metaphor is terrible, but I came up with a really good metaphor yesterday, so it's okay.) When it comes to poetry, showing up is the most important thing you can do. Show up consistently, enthusiastically, and ready to put something down on paper, even if it's the worst thing you've ever had the misfortune to read. I promise, the good stuff will come. You just have to come with it.

Another lesson my experiences with poetry have taught me is the importance of reading. If you aren't reading other people's poetry, you won't know what you like and what you don't. More importantly, if you're reading a lot of poetry, you'll have a lot of poems to respond to, which I find to be a great source of inspiration. When I first read "Tonight in Yoga" by Sierra DeMulder, I could see how it worked well with my space poem. I thought about how people connect to themselves and their universe, and specifically, how people are afraid to look inward at themselves or outward at the world because they're afraid of what they might find. The idea of the incredible vastness of space and how closely it resembles the infinite possibility of human thought led me to consider how, while space is full of light, it's also full of emptiness, just like human thought can create incredible things but can also breed extreme darkness.

This connection between looking into yourself and looking out at the world—or how introspection brings you a better relationship with the space around you—related to my original poem, as both deal with the idea of how the human mind relates to space. On the one hand, space is vast and infinite and may make it seem as if you are irrelevant, but when you look at space through yourself as a necessary part of the beauty, it becomes clear that we all belong in the world, in the universe, and in our own bodies.

Classic Poem

Tonight in Yoga
Sierra DeMulder
I realized I have been afraid of meditation my whole life,
which is to say, I have been afraid of myself my whole life,

which is to say, my whole life I have been afraid of the anti-silence
of my thoughts, which is to say, I have not been myself

my whole life, which is to say I'm sorry, which is to say my whole life
has been oh, I'm so sorry, which is to say don't mediate,

just apologize—don't worry, just be worried all the time, every day,
for your entire life that you, your heart, is broken, like an engine,

like a wine glass, like an oven you can't even stick your head in, it
  won't work right, can't
love right, but tonight, in yoga, I realized

for the first time that breathing is not the process of being filled
and emptied: breathing is the act of actually making love to

the whole world, which is to say the world is your lover, which is to say
love the whole world, in all its sweaty folds and scabbed pockmarks,

which is to say love your dirty corners, your stalk-like legs and barrel
  hips,
love all the no and the no and the no that brought you right here,

to this moment, and love the yes. The yes, the breath that found its
  way

to you, that built a home in your blood cells, changed itself

to better suit you, and for it, tonight, you say: I was made to breathe
and move and give, which is to say love. Love. I was made to love.

Response Poem

The Universe As a Metaphor
Hannah Dains

For Tuesday
"When you think about how we're hurtling through space on
      a tiny rock,
Not even the biggest in our solar system,
Dwarfed by the sun,
Which is, in turn, dwarfed by all the other stars out there,
And how one day our comparatively tiny rock
Will be swallowed by our comparatively tiny sun,
It's easy to justify slicing open your own flesh."
You said that to me once.
But my dear, space is thousands of different colors,
Blood is just one,
And we may all be made of stardust
But the galaxies inside of you are hidden so deep
That no amount of blood will reveal them,
You will never see your own nebulas, your own solar systems,
So when you're at the edge of a black hole, step away
      from the event horizon,
Because your light is so bright and so new and so beautiful.
The thing about rays is that they emanate infinitely from
      a fixed point,
And if you're behind that point

You just can't see the light that comes from every inch of
   you,
You, My dear, Are glowing.
The saddest thing about space is that it takes centuries
   for light to travel.
From the distant planets and galaxies to our eyes,
For all we know every star we see could already be gone,
   in a flash,
The light coming from something already dead,
If your light is coming from something that has already
   died years ago,
Then I want to tell you this.
You may not have come from a nebula
But both stars and people end in black holes,
No light will escape from you when you go, my friend,
No happiness, no hope,
We will simply stand at the edge trying not to fall in.
Black holes are terrifying because no one knows what's on
   the other side.
I don't know what's inside of you,
What planets and asteroids and constellations you are
   hiding,
But I've seen what comes out. And what it leaves behind.
You said you wanted your body to be a map of the galaxies,
But space is not a straight line.
Your scars look nothing like the universe.

Get Writing

Look in.

1. What do you discover about yourself when you find old things you've made or written?
2. Is there anything you'd be willing to practice for ten thousand hours? What is it? Why?
3. Has a friend ever inspired your best work? How?
4. Write about a time when you got something you really wanted. How did getting it feel?
5. Explore a time when you found people that felt like your tribe or your kind.

SHOUT out.

1. Try writing a terrible poem. Use cliché metaphors. Clunky language. Bad grammar.
2. Now find something unexpected in that poem and transform it into something you like.

Claim your classic.

Classic Poems about Friendship, Encouragement, and Offering Love

"Allons! The road is before us . . ." from "Song of the Open Road," Walt Whitman

"Failing and Flying," Jack Gilbert

"Hug O' War," Shel Silverstein

"[i carry your heart with me(i, carry it in]" E. E. Cummings

"I'm Nobody! Who Are You?" Emily Dickinson

"If You Were Still Around," Sam Shepard
"maggie and milly and molly and may," E. E. Cummings
"No Man Is an Island," John Donne
"The Big Heart," Anne Sexton
"Ways of Talking," Ha Jin

6
QUEER
ADRIAN KLJUCEC, 18

Adrian's Story

I remember when I was in ninth grade and my father got diagnosed with stage 3 cancer after my mother had already beaten breast cancer twice. Within the same couple of months, my mom quit her job of twenty-seven years because there was a change in management when her longtime boss died. We were facing a threat from our landlord to evict us, and I hadn't come out as trans yet; I was still presenting as a feminine female.

I am a genderqueer, nonbinary, transmasculine individual, and I use he/him/his and they/them/theirs pronouns. I was born and raised in the heart of Los Angeles.

I struggled with depression my whole life, and during this year, it got much worse. I was dealing with anxiety and had suicidal thoughts every day. I just didn't feel right. Something was wrong. Something had *always* been wrong, but I couldn't figure it out. I thought I might be a lesbian. Nope, tried that—it wasn't me. I began expressing myself in a very butch/ masculine way, and although that felt the closer to my real self, something was still off. Finally, a friend who had begun transitioning told me about his experience. He opened me up to resources and others in the trans community, and I finally understood that I wasn't actually a girl.

At first, I came out as male, but after the first year of my transition, I realized that I was nonbinary (neither male nor female). There are more genders than our society recognizes (so far, it only recognizes two: male and female). I finally came out as trans when I was fifteen, at the beginning of my junior year in high school. This helped me in one way but made things harder in another, as I faced new kinds of discrimination and violence.

At this point, I had been writing for a couple of years and dreamed of attending Brave New Voices (the national teen poetry competition) or joining Get Lit—someplace where I was safe and could actively write and be involved with a community. I joined Get Lit and attended Brave New Voices as a poet on the Get Lit team, writing about my addiction to alcohol and how I got sober at the age of fifteen. I wrote about my transition and my trans experience. I wanted to reach other queer youth and youth who were struggling with addiction. I wanted to be the voice that found them when they thought no such voice existed. I knew what it was like to feel alone like that, absolutely isolated—that I was less worthy of love than anyone else. It's easy to internalize the cissexism and antiqueerness present in our hetero-patriarchal culture. I had experienced it.

At the end of high school and the beginning of college, I was also in several unhealthy relationships. I never talked about it. Nobody knew— not even me. I just knew that I was in a lot of pain. A counselor at my new university helped me see the pattern and also helped me recognize problems I had with my father. These were huge revelations for me, but they brought painful memories to the surface. I was hurt and confused and scared. I felt terribly lost.

During these years, I was also dealing with the repercussions of concussions I sustained while playing soccer in high school. I had played for eight years, but during my sophomore year, I got six concussions. The concussions resulted in brain damage and post-concussion syndrome, which heightened my ADHD. This made the rest of high school even more of a nightmare for me than it already had been. Once I graduated and got diagnosed, I started taking steps to address my challenges.

I am still dealing with the trauma from that time in my life. It's been a long journey to self-love, and although I've made a lot of progress, I still have a long way to go.

Walt Whitman's "To You" is a love poem, and my "Queer Bodies" is also a love poem—one for my girlfriend, for myself, for queerness, and for the revolution. There are many similarities and parallels between these pieces. Whitman expresses true appreciation and admiration for the person he is speaking to. He speaks of their physical features as authentic and remarkable over everyone else's. My poem is an empowering piece about queerness and queer bodies, because our bodies are policed, harassed, shamed, assaulted, and "tolerated." The importance and meaning of queer bodies is not recognized. We are perceived as *less than*, and we often internalize this. This piece holds queer bodies above science and religion, which have been used to delegitimize our existence. Liberating queerness and queer bodies means resisting assimilation, a theme in both poems.

I am very grateful to be a part of Get Lit, to have gotten out of Los Angeles, and to be attending college and getting an incredible education. Although my campus is more progressive and safer than others, it is not an ideal place for queer students, students of color, students who are differently abled, or students who have to face any type of marginalization. I have taken a very active role on campus to address these issues and create a safer, more inclusive and accessible campus. My passion is social justice, and I definitely see myself working in this field in the future.

Classic Poem

From "To You" in Leaves of Grass by Walt Whitman

Whoever you are, I fear you are walking the walks of dreams,

I fear these supposed realities are to melt from under your feet and
*   hands,*

Even now, your features, joys, speech, house, trade, manners, troubles,
*   follies, costume, crimes dissipate away from you,*

Your true soul and body appear before me,

They stand forth out of affairs, out of commerce, shops, work, farms,
*   clothes, the house, buying, selling, eating, drinking, suffering,*
*   dying.*

Whoever you are, now I place my hand upon you, that you be my
*   poem,*

I whisper with my lips close to your ear,

I have loved many women and men, but I love none better than you.

O I have been dilatory and dumb,

I should have made my way straight to you long ago,

I should have blabb'd nothing but you, I should have chanted nothing
*   but you.*

I will leave all and come and make the hymns of you,

None has understood you, but I understand you,

None has done justice to you, you have not done justice to yourself,

None but has found you imperfect, I only find no imperfection in you,

None but would subordinate you, I only am he who will never consent
*   to subordinate you,*

I only am he who places over you no master, owner, better, God,
*   beyond what waits intrinsically in yourself . . .*

O I could sing such grandeurs and glories about you!
You have not known what you are, you have slumber'd upon yourself
all your life,
Your eyelids have been the same as closed most of the time,
What you have done returns already in mockeries,
(Your thrift, knowledge, prayers, if they do not return in mockeries,
what is their return?)

The mockeries are not you,
Underneath them and within them I see you lurk,
I pursue you where none else has pursued you,
Silence, the desk, the flippant expression, the night, the accustom'd
routine, if these conceal you from others or from yourself, they do
not conceal you from me,
The shaved face, the unsteady eye, the impure complexion, if these
balk others they do not balk me,
The pert apparel, the deform'd attitude, drunkenness, greed, prema-
ture death, all these I part aside.

There is no endowment in man or woman that is not tallied in you,
There is no virtue, no beauty in man or woman, but as good is in you,
No pluck, no endurance in others, but as good is in you,
No pleasure waiting for others, but an equal pleasure waits for you.

As for me, I give nothing to any one except I give the like carefully
to you,
I sing the songs of the glory of none, not God, sooner than
I sing the songs of the glory of you . . .

Response Poem

Your Body
Adrian Kljucec

Your body is not an apology.

It is every miracle.

It is the flame on top of a cancer patient's last birthday
cake.

Your body is not a wish. It is the shooting star.

Your body is peace. It is the end to war.

Your body is the answer to the question Life poses.

It is every single fantasy come to life.
It shows me all that is true.
Everything that is magic.

It is a prayer. It is a sacred text.
Your body is a capital B. It is the divine.
It is religious. It is spiritual. It is my Bible. It is my Torah. It
is my Quran.
And the scary part is, I'm not even religious.

I am not body positive, I am body honest. And your body is
honesty. Your body is the truest form of beauty. I find
no deception in your skin.

Your body is an experience.
One that I want to share with you, that I want to cherish
    and never forget.

Your body is desire.

Your body is a poem.
I want to read it every day, I want to memorize it.
I want to close my eyes and recite it. I want to feel it when
    there's nothing left to feel.

Your body is an oasis. It is the sun at the end of forever.

Even when I go blind from your body's light, I will fall deeper
    in love with the sacred prayers your goose bumps will
    have printed in Braille. I get lost in your body's promises
    and forget that the world is a failed mosaic. That we
    do not fit in the world's frame.

Your body is the big bang. Fuck its theory, your body is proof.

Your body is heaven. It is the galaxy. It is the entire universe.

I don't need scripture, or formulas, or evidence; your body
    has every reason for me to believe.

Your body is Queer and the most comfortable thing to me.

Get Writing

Look in.

1. Did you ever have a delayed reaction to something painful? What was it? Why couldn't you face it in the moment?
2. In what ways do you feel uncomfortable in your own skin?
3. Has anyone ever mistreated you? How could you protect yourself from this in the future?
4. Are there any memories you hide from?
5. What has your journey toward self-love looked like? Are you there yet?

SHOUT out.

1. Respond to Adrian's poem "Your Body." Write a poem called "Your Body" to yourself or to someone else.
2. Find one line from Adrian's poem and riff off it.

Claim your classic.

Classic Poems for Self-Acceptance, Loving Others, and Owning Your Place in the World

"A Supermarket in California," Allen Ginsberg
"How Does It Feel to Be a Heart?" Hafiz
"Belly Song," Etheridge Knight
"Buoyancy," Rumi
"Those Sundays," Christopher Soto (Loma)
"Jewelry Store," Andrea Gibson
"Nebraska," Miles Walser

"Poem (Let Us Live)," Joshua Jennifer Espinoza
"Queer," Frank Bidart
"Unfold Your Own Myth," Rumi

7

Remind yourself nobody built like you, you designed yourself.

—Jay Z

NUMB

KYLAND TURNER, 18

Kyland's Story

The first time I heard my dad's voice, I was five. He and my mom were fighting, and I could barely hear him over *The Miseducation of Lauryn Hill*. When my mom found out she was pregnant, she was only sixteen—and this was way before shows like *Teen Mom* made teen pregnancy look glamorous. There were no endorsements, no reality TV deals. From the time I was born until I started pre-K, our reality was that we were homeless and living in shelters. Eventually, we moved to South LA, a neighborhood made for unwanted youth. There was no hope, no opportunities, but plenty of accessible drugs and guns. I vaguely remember the day my dad finally moved in, but I vividly remember the day he moved out. Then five years went by without hearing from him. You can imagine how that affected me as an adolescent.

I was constantly getting jumped, I couldn't focus in school, and I started to self-medicate and make bad choices. I was diagnosed with ADHD the same day I got a call saying my grandma wasn't doing so well. I had just seen her the day before, but she passed that night. I was devastated. She had raised me since I was young, and before I could even process her death, I lost one of my closest friends to gang violence. These are the stories I write in my notebook now that I know how to turn my pain into art.

I didn't start processing my emotions until I was seventeen. Before that, suicide weighed heavily on my mind, and by fifteen, I had dropped out of school to become involved in a lifestyle that would either lead to an early death or to prison. My mom would tell me I was on a destructive path, but I didn't care. When I was arrested, that was the first sign I had to change my life. That's when I made the decision to return to school, and began recording my struggle through poetry and rap. After working to be the best at my craft, I was noticed by Get Lit—Words Ignite.

As a Get Lit Player, I perform classic poetry like "The Survivor" by Tadeusz Różewicz. I can relate to the poem because I have lost friends and family to violent deaths, and I have encountered situations where I have almost lost my life to my own hands. Everything that I went through I still survived, and that is what inspired me to write my response poem "Yesterday I was 12." I realized that I had a story to tell and a story that needed to be heard. In this poem, I just want to show people that no matter what they go through, it doesn't define them, make them, or break them. Like the quote by the ancient Roman poet Ovid, I encourage you to "be patient and tough; someday this pain may be useful to you."

I read and respond to classical poetry for youth who might be going through the same problems that I did and are looking for a way out. Not a performance goes by without a student coming up to me and telling me they could relate to what I said. I also work to inspire my school, where I cofounded a leadership club called Men of Excellence. In order to participate in special events, every member needs to maintain a GPA above 2.5.

I work hard to mentor my peers and encourage them to listen to their teachers, make up their work, and stay after school. My own grades have gone up since I started focusing on becoming a better performer. When I saw my last report card full of As and Bs, it felt like I was dreaming.

Life still feels like a dream. Over the past few months, I have been invited to perform at Dodger Stadium, the Professional Musicians' Union in Hollywood, and at the Actors Hall of Fame. I was even chosen to be an ABC News "Cool Kid." After being awarded a scholarship, I was interviewed about my poetry and the work I do to motivate my peers. It's amazing to think this is now my life when, only five years ago, I was considering ending it all. Now I have something to live for. I want to go to college so I can show other kids that no matter what you go through, you can *be something*. All it takes is belief in yourself and the willingness to pursue excellence.

Classic Poem

The Survivor
Tadeusz Różewicz
I am twenty-four
led to slaughter
I survived.

The following are empty synonyms:
man and beast
love and hate
friend and foe
darkness and light.

The way of killing men and beasts is the same
I've seen it:
truckfuls of chopped-up men
who will not be saved.

Ideas are mere words:
virtue and crime
truth and lies
beauty and ugliness
courage and cowardice.

Virtue and crime weigh the same
I've seen it:
in a man who was both
criminal and virtuous.
I seek a teacher and a master
may he restore my sight, hearing, and speech

may he again name objects and ideas
may he separate darkness from light.

I am twenty-four
led to slaughter
I survived.

Response Poem

Yesterday I Was 12
Kyland Turner

My 18th birthday just passed and I began to reflect on
    the past
On how life moves so fast because
Yesterday I was 12
I remember puberty was at its beginning stage
A couple hairs was growing
A couple muscles was showing
It was yesterday when I was coming home from watching
Welcome Home, Roscoe Jenkins and I got a call
From my mom saying, "Your grandma isn't doing too fine"
It was yesterday when it had been two years since I seen
    my dad
And all I wanted was a phone call
It was yesterday when the doctors came in
Saying, "We have a diagnosis for your son"
Because yesterday my money was as low as my pants
So I did what I thought was a man
It was yesterday when I seen my best friend take his last
    breath
It was yesterday when I was all alone

My mom was home
but her mind wasn't home
It was yesterday when a teacher crushed my preteen
   dreams
'Cause yesterday I thought I could drink the pain away
But I found the pain never went away
In fact it stayed
So yesterday I began to cut my wrist with a blade
And that same blade was being held by the devil's hand
You see, I was only 12 when along with my grandma
My hopes and dreams died
I cried and cried
I was only 12 when all I wanted was my dad to call
I wondered did he want to be bothered at all
I was only 12 when the doctors said I had ADHD—they tried
   to fix me
With this little pink thing
They tried to kill my raw zeal
A robot they tried to build
I was only 12 when my first drug sell
Was to a girl with a life forming inside of her but this other
   side of her
Had that life deforming
I was only 12 when I seen my best friend take his last breath
He was right next to me
So an angel must have been next to me
'Cause I should have died that day
I was only 12 when all I wanted was
Love but my mom was too busy grieving in the club
I was only 12 when a teacher told me,
"You will never make it past 17"

I was only 12 when I was a statistic from the absence of
    black man
I was only 12 when Hennessy became my remedy
Suicide was heavy on my mind
The devil tried to steal my soul
But today I picked up a bible
And it told me to hold on and stay strong
Because it was yesterday when
Puberty was at its beginning stage
A couple hairs was growing
A couple muscles was showing
Yesterday I was 12
But today...I'm 18.

Get Writing

Look in.

1. Has anyone ever left your life in an incomprehensible way? Who?
   How did you cope?
2. Which feelings are you trying to numb? What are you numbing them
   with? The internet? Your phone? Food? Drugs? Alcohol? What do
   you think would happen if you didn't numb them?
3. Have you ever had a moment when you knew you needed to change
   some aspect of your life in a major way? Which moment was it?
4. In what ways have you learned to pursue excellence?

SHOUT out.

1. Write your own poem "Yesterday I Was [fill in the blank]" about an age in your life that was critical in making you who you are.
2. Write about a time when you felt someone was trying to fix you. What were they trying to fix?

Claim your classic.

Classic Poems for Being Fatherless, for Perseverance, for Accepting Yourself, and for Finding Joy Amid Adversity

"A Dream Deferred," Langston Hughes

"A Story that Could Be True," William Stafford

"Everybody's Something," Chance the Rapper

"I Am Learning to Abandon the World," Linda Pastan

"I Had Been Hungry All the Years," Emily Dickinson

"Last Night As I Was Sleeping," Antonio Machado

"My Papa's Waltz," Theodore Roethke

"The Boy Died in My Alley," Gwendolyn Brooks

"The Little Orphan," Edgar Albert Guest

"Waiting for Icarus," Muriel Rukeyser

BLACK SHEEP

JESSICA ROMOFF, 15

Jessica's Story

I haven't really been thinking about it much, but I have changed DRA-MATICALLY in the past three years of my life. I was talking to my seventh-grade English teacher, Mr. Trivas, asking how in the entire universe was I going to even attempt to write "my story." Do I even have a story? What the hell is *my story*? I don't think I'm actually interesting enough to have "a story." Nevertheless, I'm sure everyone has a story, and I guess that means I have one too.

From kindergarten to around sixth grade, I had a pretty mainstream childhood. I played sports, did fine in school, and had a decent amount of friends. I can't remember having a reason to not be happy, so I guess my parents did a pretty successful job (they did an amazing job). The only blemish or smudge was that my mom and I fought like crazy—well, we still do. I think it has something to do with her being extremely overprotective and me never listening to her. It's hard to put our relationship into words—whenever I try, it never sounds like I'm explaining it correctly. Oh, and the amount of poems I have attempted to convey it in is really astounding but also kind of depressing because I have not yet succeeded. Like I want to write and read and dye my hair pink, and she wants me to run for class president or be on the debate team. I'm never really going to be what she hoped/predicted while cradling me all bloody with her hair plastered to her forehead, sweaty from childbirth. But that's why she had my sister—someone predictable and most likely to join debate team or run for class president.

Anyway, my life from sixth grade and before was nothing really interesting to write about. I was just like everyone else: loud, obnoxious, didn't brush my teeth, patiently waiting for something to fill my bra cup. The start of middle school was when I began to hit speed bumps. If there is one underlying moral in my middle school story, it's probably that thirteen-year-old girls are Satan's elves and that I was a stupid twig.

So what happened was that I was knotted in this toxic friend group of girls who knew I was pretty much weak. They figured out how they could torment me because I was (am) sensitive and fragile—I always have been that way. They would exclude me, gossip about me, and blame me for problems that I had nothing to do with. But I still latched on to them, and apologized and cried for their forgiveness. Ugh, such a stupid twig.

In middle school, once we had outgrown and shed the "cooties" thing, all anyone wanted was a boyfriend. One weekend, I was at this bat-mitzva party, and my "friends" were ignoring me as usual, running away from me. And then this boy who they all were apparently "in love" with asked me to be his girlfriend (HA-HA-HA-HA-HA). And I said yes in the heat of the moment; no one had ever shown interest in me before.

So that one simple yes was how I lost all of my friends! The girls spread rumors about me, ignored me, and made sure that anyone else who I had ever been friends with hated me as well. I had zero friends—

no one liked me, and people even began to use words like "slut" and "whore." I WAS A SEVENTH GRADER! And that's how my depression started, I think.

I remember that weekend. All I wanted to do was die, and I slept for, like, two days straight and didn't eat. I had no one. I remember everything looked grayer, and I began to think about suicide. A suicidal seventh grader—the memories still bring me to tears. I was so innocent and helpless. And let me remind you that this was all because I said yes to a boy wanting to be my boyfriend.

The problems with my mom got worse because I was acting out and becoming really reckless and impulsive; it's not like I could talk to her about it. She'd say something about how I was ruining our family's reputation and how I was ruining *my* reputation. (It's really interesting how the thought of reputation dissolves when death consumes 50 percent of your thoughts.) I had no idea how to channel my emotions, so I remember breaking things like pencil boxes and ripping apart books. I couldn't sleep either.

But then, after every storm, the sun will eventually break through. I still remember this exact day perfectly. Seventh-grade English class, last track of the day. Mr. Trivas was talking about poetry and "the spoken word" (whatever *that* meant), and he was showing us videos that I found boring and insignificant. The last video he put up was a spoken-word poem called "Perfect" by Maia Mayor. I remember it felt like I had been hit by a large moving vehicle of some sort. I got goose bumps all over, and when it was finished, I started crying as I left the classroom. My teacher asked if I was okay, and for the first time, I said no.

I'm crying as I'm writing this (happy tears!) because I really have no idea where I would be right now if he hadn't shown us Maia's poem. After nearly five months of being alone, misunderstood, and feeling like I was the only one in the entire world who felt like this, there was finally someone who understood me. Human relation felt so foreign. And then something really weird happened. My mood lifted. I slept better. My grades actually improved. I stopped breaking things and shifted to expressing with a pen and paper. It was such a beautiful thing, really. Poetry became my medication, I guess you could say. I'd heard of people smoking and drinking to self-medicate, but I didn't need that to fix me on bad days because writing and poetry did.

I memorized Maia's poem and would recite it in the shower and stuff when I was angry. And then I'd feel better. Interesting, right? I'd *feel* better.

A few months later, Get Lit came to our school and Maia read "Perfect" in person (and of course, I cried). But I remember thinking how impossible it would be for me to ever do something like that. Mr. Trivas said that when I was older, I could try out for GetLit, but that sounded the same as him saying that when I was older, I could run for president of the United States or something.

Nevertheless, in eighth grade, I began reading at the open mics. I would get all jittery on the car ride there and would spend all week trying to memorize poems. And I loved the way it felt to read them, even in front of the twenty people or less who were there. My knees would shake and my hands would shiver, and it felt like electricity was swimming through my bloodstream. I'd feel this rattling in my ears afterward. I have terrible stage fright, but who cared when it gave me this rush? (The rush was actually from the stage fright!) I also stopped being so reckless and looking for things to make me feel alive because that's what reading poetry felt like. Reading poetry felt like being alive.

For example, when I first read Ann Sexton's poem "Her Kind," there was something about it that made me think, *Wow, this is a strong woman.* The speaker in the poem seemed to have been rejected by society and wandered off on her own in the woods. And even through that oppression, the ending stanza has a fire to it (when I read it, I get chills). So after I read the poem, I realized how I felt the complete opposite: I *wasn't* a strong woman. So I wrote the poem "Manners" to illustrate why and how I felt small—nothing like Sexton. But at the end of my poem, I empowered myself by saying, "I've been teaching myself now." I feel stronger now!

At the end of eighth grade, my classmates elected me to write the graduation speech. It's so strange because I didn't even associate myself with writing until I was exposed to spoken-word poetry. Then, when ninth grade finally came, I tried out to become a Get Lit Player, and after a few months, I made it.

Get Lit is that one thing I look forward to, to get me through the week. It's an amazing break from all the stupid and shallow people in my community; I get to spend my Saturdays with roughly eight extremely intelligent and gifted writers. They have all become my role models. But I didn't even know any of them at the beginning!

My depression has gotten increasingly better, and I feel like I owe a lot of my recovery to Get Lit. I actually have no idea where I'd be right now without it. I could have started using drugs or drinking or something. Maybe dropped out of school? Get Lit really turned me away from negative possibilities—got me back on the right course.

What I would like to give back to the world is something similar to what Maia gave me. I haven't written a good enough poem yet, but when I do, I really hope that one seventh-grade girl loosens her shoulders, sighs, and thinks, *She understands me.*

I have now written my story.

Classic Poem

Her Kind
Anne Sexton

I have gone out, a possessed witch,
haunting the black air, braver at night;
dreaming evil, I have done my hitch
over the plain houses, light by light:
lonely thing, twelve-fingered, out of mind.
A woman like that is not a woman, quite.
I have been her kind.

I have found the warm caves in the woods,
filled them with skillets, carvings, shelves,
closets, silks, innumerable goods;
fixed the suppers for the worms and the elves:
whining, rearranging the disaligned.
A woman like that is misunderstood.
I have been her kind.

I have ridden in your cart, driver,
waved my nude arms at villages going by,
learning the last bright routes, survivor
where your flames still bite my thigh
and my ribs crack where your wheels wind.
A woman like that is not ashamed to die.
I have been her kind.

Response Poem

Manners
Jessica Romoff

My mom always taught me
That it's easier just to say sorry
To say please and thank you

Occasionally, no thank you. I was force-fed table manners,
Phrases like, "When you have nothing nice to say, don't say
     anything."
"Don't use the word 'hate'; instead say, 'I don't care for,'"
"And remember to say 'Sorry,' even when it's not your fault."
I carried each of my mother's syllables with the loose
     change in my pockets,
Held them under my tongue and between clenched jaws.

Luckily, I haven't been in too many other situations where
     I've had to stray from one of those phrases.
There was just this one time,
When I was at a party and this guy
Kept coming up to me
And he kept touching me and pulling on my arm
And I was trying to push him off, but that wasn't working
And I had no idea what to do
Then he said I was just a stupid slut in front of everyone
     there.

And the only words that would fit in my mouth
That my tongue could wrap around

The only words that I could whisper into the empty stomach
        of the room was, "I'm sorry."
All I could say was, "I'm sorry."

It felt like he was sliding my self-worth back into my
        pockets
Like he was hemming my lips over themselves, teaching my
        helplessness.
And all I could hear was my mom telling me to put my napkin
        on my lap
To remember to say please and thank you
And all I could remember was
If I had nothing nice to say,
Don't say anything at all.
Do not say anything at all.

My mom never told me that sometimes the right word is,
        "No,"
Is, "Leave me alone,"
Is, "Don't touch me,"
Is using your knuckles instead of a quivering throat.
My mom never told me that sometimes I'm going to have to
        forget my table manners,
That I'm gonna have to eat with my fingers,
That I am going to hate,
That I'm gonna get dirt in my nails sometimes.

I've been teaching myself now...
Getting better at looking people in the eyes
Learning how to grit my teeth,
Not needing to keep one hand on the phone

And the other on the pepper spray
When I'm alone.

'Cause I have faith in my bones,
'Cause I have faith in my shoulders and my knees,
And I don't need to keep saying I'm sorry
When I have a pair of lungs and a tongue
That works just fine.

Get Writing

Look in.

1. Have you ever felt shut out or cut off by friends?
2. Do you ever feel like you are not who or what your parents want you to be?
3. Did you ever have something good but felt like you couldn't enjoy it because it would make someone else feel bad?
4. Was there ever a time when you thought your life was meaningless and later realized you made a huge difference to someone else? Like Maia did for Jessica?

SHOUT out.

1. Tell the story of a time you fought with a parent.
2. Pick a part of Jessica's poem "Manners" that helps you understand something you hadn't understood before. Use that part to write about how no one understands you or to explore some part of you that is misunderstood or rejected.

3. Write a poem about what you have but don't deserve or what you deserve but don't have.

Claim your classic.

Classic Poems on Being Cut Off, Heeding Your Own Voice, Finding a Sense of Self, and Feeling Young

"A Sad Child," Margaret Atwood

"Everything Is Waiting for You," David Whyte

"For a Daughter Who Leaves," Janice Mirikitani

"Green, Green Is My Sister's House," Mary Oliver

"Sweet Darkness," David Whyte

"The Borders," Sharon Olds

"To Women As Far As I'm Concerned," D. H. Lawrence

"The Fury of Rainstorms," Anne Sexton

"The Lost Jewel," Emily Dickinson

"They Was Girls Together," Cherríe Moraga

SPECTRUM

IAN KOHN, 14

Ian's Story

Attuned to the sounds of words by nature, I was told, starting at around first grade, that I was inherently gifted with expression. However, I did not acquire the same passion for words as I have today until around seventh grade. I was considered throughout the majority of my life to be eccentric and nonsocial due to having Asperger's syndrome.

When I was younger and didn't know about my Asperger's, I imagined that the reason I acted differently than others was because everyone but me had something interesting up their sleeves. A general dislike for the commonplace began to spawn within me, which I still have today and will never wane as long as I continue to express myself. I believe that my words are the key to my advancement in life, since creativity cannot be shown unless it is communicated.

My head is not so far up in the clouds anymore, though I wish I could get away with it now.

In middle school my social problems became more acutely obvious to me and writing became an avid hobby. I learned of Asperger's syndrome and its effects, and I became so psychologically repulsed by my social incapacities that I set out to reform myself. I set myself apart from others so that they would have no choice but to want to find out more about my interests and befriend me. I did so by availing myself of the so-called "way with words" I was said to have.

But I still could not become absorbed in a book as easily as I could a video game, so I decided to rigorously memorize word definitions, resulting in my tendency to frequently use long words in my writing and speaking. I'm sure you, the reader, can figure out how well this was received at school. People began to view me as a living dictionary who could probe written works better than anyone else. I practiced my talent with words by first writing short prose, then poetry. I dabbled in the sesquipedalian works of nineteenth-century authors like Edgar Allan Poe. Of these, I stuck with poetry because of the accessibility and leeway it gives to fledgling writers, as well as poetry's embrace of divergent thought. I eventually decided that I wanted to pursue writing as a possible career.

Meanwhile, I was still struggling socially. I began to avoid interactions just to pen stories and poems, mainly because I still did not know how to start or maintain a conversation. By the end of seventh grade, I became ostracized by two best friends, making me feel bereft of friends entirely. In the eighth grade my parents enrolled me in PEERS (Program for the Education and Enrichment of Relational Skills) social-skills classes. These taught me the bare bones of interrelational dynamics, for which I am indebted, but they did not succeed in helping me befriend people at the largest institution I am involved in: school.

All this changed, however, when a fellow PEERS student told me about Get Lit—Words Ignite, a spoken-word, poetry-related nonprofit organization that focuses on helping students create poems inspired by eminent poets of the past. I eagerly joined the program, infatuated with the idea of honing my craft collaboratively and making friends at the same time. I had no experience with spoken-word poetry, but I learned quickly. I gave my first public reading at a bullying-themed workshop and eventually did an open-mic performance.

I finally found a place where I could successfully befriend others. Whereas memorizing the dictionary was seen as a joke at school, a trait of an outcast, the poets of Get Lit embraced every inch of my eccentricity and encouraged me to tell it to the world. Over the course of four months, I honed my craft until I came to the attention of the founder of Get Lit, Diane, who asked me to audition for a spot on a team for the Classic Slam. I was ecstatic! My team placed third overall—a feat of great magnitude, especially considering how some teams had an entire semester to prepare. We had done it in a matter of weeks.

I am indebted to Get Lit for showing me how eloquence, especially within children, can lead to sociopolitical change, as well as changes from within the soul to around the world. I believe that being a part of it has given me a purpose in a life—a purpose for which I struggled for a long time. My struggles have given me subjects to write about, which will inspire others to interact with and stop discriminating against those who have Asperger's Syndrome. One of the most common topics of my spoken word poetry at the moment are my struggles with social interactions and how they do not make me any less of a human being.

I affirm this belief in my response to D. H. Lawrence's "Women Want Fighters for Their Lovers," a classic poem that I took offense to due to its statement that machismo invariably attracts would-be lovers (be them male, female, or not of the gender binary). No persona should be donned to attract people since the best person one can be is oneself.

Classic Poem

Women Want Fighters for Their Lovers
D. H. Lawrence

Women don't want wistful
mushy, pathetic young men
struggling in doubtful embraces
then trying again.

Mushy and treacherous, tiny
Peterlets, Georgelets, Hamlets,
Tomlets, Dicklets, Harrylets, whiney
Jimlets and self-sorry Samlets.

Women are sick of consoling
inconsolable youth, dead-beat;
pouring comfort and condoling
down the sink of the male conceit.

Women want fighters, fighters
and the fighting cock.
Can't you give it them, blighters!

The fighting cock, the fighting cock—
Have you got one, little blighters?
Let it crow then, like one o'clock!

Response Poem

Intergender Relations
Ian Kohn

If a fighter is what a lady wishes to obtain,

then I say I'm fighting a war within myself

just to coax my conscience to let me say to them more than
    merely a dismissive "Hi,"

as if I believe that truthfully I am a blighter amounting to
    little more than

the soot a damsel scrapes off her labor boots, without a
    care at all

if she hurt its body or feelings if it were a living being.

In fact, I'd wager to say that that's exactly how I'm left
    feeling

when a girl I wish to court walks away after refusing an
    offer to partake in small talk

because I'm socially inept,

She fears small talk is the basis for an in-depth conversation
    and then a friendship—

That, and a mourning, inconsolable chill that spawns in my
    stomach

tells me no one will ever care to get to know I have

distinctiveness.

No, I was not being a tiny Peterlet having a panic attack

in my cerebrum, because I'm six feet tall, and my
    confidence

was enough to enable me to greet her.

Nor am I narcissistic and implying that I'm what I

would call a male equivalent to arm candy.

But I feel now that any person of the female gender can
        at least look beyond
the shyness embodied in this Autistic Spectrum facade
and acknowledge the fact that your trends are not my
        trends, I would rather insist
that the big bang happened due to sheer coincidence
        than accept
the hypocritical word of God, and that what you see as a
pointless school assignment I see as a further step toward
        an incommensurable future.
But if you insist keenly that I take to honing my biceps and
        pectoral muscles to become
a veritable knight covered in skin-deep armor so that when
        I hug someone, they feel
might and not affection, you know as much about romance
        as girls know about me.
And now, I'm accustomed to being cleaved to the seating
        of a bench
five meters away from a love interest's flesh during lunch
        period, and I try to eat my
meal and hope that the most meager look at her can be
        snatched
without her spotting me and speculating that I—with her
        consent—wish to "get funky."
To me, affection will never lie in tapping a lady's ass, but
        rather
gliding my aether extremities up the epidermal layer of a
        mistress's hips,
which are connected to an ample posterior,
relishing every bit of her existence, with the magnum opus
        being a mind that connects

to my own like an electrical outlet to a plug,
a seeming impossibility with regard to a me and another
    male.
And then, I tell her, with a burgundy heart full of the
    intention not of consummation,
but of unification, let us be together, unlike any relation-
    ship anyone can have with me,
least of all most of the boys my age that I have
    encountered.
Whereas they will talk glibly about lewdness and television
    shows deemed masculine,
a girl will generally fuse her speech with raw emotion,
so long as you respect her in return.

Being beautiful is just a stepping stone toward interest.
Being smart is the capstone of the temple of a relationship
    with me.
Being out of a relationship just ensures that I will still be a
    fighter
fighting for the possibility
of befriending you.

Get Writing

Look in.

1. Where does your faith come from?
2. How are you different?
3. Who understands the real you?

4. Which relationship skills do you have? Which do you lack?
5. Do you find it easy or difficult to attract others to you? Why?

SHOUT out.

1. Write about a fight you're fighting within yourself.
2. Take a line from Ian's poem "Intergender Relations" and use it to inspire a poem of your own.

Claim your classic.

Classic Poems for Being Different, Defying Facades, Finding Acceptance, and Fighting the System

"All I Ask," D. H. Lawrence

"Alone," Edgar Allan Poe

"Boy at the Window," Richard Wilbur

"I Cry," Tupac Shakur

"Joe, I Never Write About You," Jose Antonio Rodriguez

"Mrs. Caldera's House of Things," Gregory Djanikian

"next to of course god america i," E. E. Cummings

"Ode to My Suit," Pablo Neruda

"A.D.D.," Rafael Casal

"They Never Send Sam to the Store Anymore," Jack Prelutsky

> Don't repay evil for evil. Don't retaliate when people say unkind things about you. Instead, pay them back with a blessing. That is what God wants you to do, and he will bless you for it.
>
> **—Peter 3:9**

HAVE-NOT

MARQUESHA BABERS, 19

Marquesha's Story

I sometimes wake up early in the morning and think back on my life. I just think about everything I've been through, good and bad. It helps me appreciate the way my life is now. Even though there are still some things that sometimes make me feel like the world is falling down around me, I am very grateful that things are not how they used to be. I have had a lifetime full of traumatizing events.

My childhood ended at eight years old, when my family and I became homeless. It was my mother, my older brother, my baby brother, and me. We were never stable. I attended three different elementary schools, five different middle schools, and four different high schools.

I used to love going to school—but not because of friends, because I didn't have friends. I just loved going to school because I loved knowing. I asked questions every day. I wondered about things that no third grader would ever wonder. Knowledge was so interesting to me and still is, but after my first year of middle school, I slowly began to hate school. Not only was I getting bullied on a daily basis and had no one there for me, but I also felt as if I was not gaining the knowledge that I was supposed to.

It was in the middle of my sixth-grade year that, due to our homelessness, we were forced to move and I had to switch schools again. On the first day, I walked into my first class and the teacher told me, "Welcome to hell. I am mad, so I will be giving the class hell." I was shocked and scared. That was the first time in my life that I felt like I did not want to go to school anymore, but my hunger for knowledge helped me to look past her ignorance—at first. Eventually, though, this and the other daily challenges overtook my love of school.

I have always been an extremely nice person, which was not necessarily a good thing. I grew up with two brothers, and we were sheltered children. My mom always told us that all we had was each other, and because of our homelessness, I had an issue with attachment. I was the total opposite of people with attachment issues who wouldn't want to get close to others. I would want to get as close to people as possible, as fast as possible because I never knew when or how long I would be around that person. I wanted to have as many memories of people as I could because I felt that if I didn't have these memories, people would never remember me. That's why I really fell in love with poetry; with it, people will always have something to remember me by.

I was so nice and naive that I was taken advantage of in more ways than one. People never took me seriously; they only took things from me, and to me, that was love and friendship. When I was nine years old, I found out that the world wasn't the nice place I had once believed it to be. I was raped while my mom was working the graveyard shift at her job. My life was forever changed. To make the burden even harder for me to carry, I didn't tell anyone about it for two years—not even my mother.

That is why Sonia's poem "Song No. 2" speaks to me so much. "I say to all you young girls molested at ten"—this line spoke to my soul the very first time I read it. I felt as though she was talking to me directly, and in a weird way, she was. I had claimed her poem as my own and carried her words on my hip.

I was inspired by Sonia's ferocity to write my own response poem. I had held it in me for a long time, but one day, when the boy I talk about in the poem wrote me on Facebook like nothing had ever happened, I got really mad, but instead of acting out of anger, I wrote this poem.

I want people to know that they are beautiful no matter what has happened to them or what anyone says, and I also want them to know that sometimes the same person who's hurt you could be the same person who's begging you to like them. Writing and performing "You Said" absolutely helped me get over certain things in my childhood, and it has really saved me. Words can heal whether they come from you or from someone else. Never be afraid to claim your poem.

Classic Poem

Song No. 2
Sonia Sanchez

(1)

i say. all you young girls waiting to live
i say. all you young girls taking yo pill
i say. all you sisters tired of standing still
i say. all you sisters thinkin you won't, but you will.

don't let them kill you with their stare
don't let them closet you with no air
don't let them feed you sex piecemeal
don't let them offer you any old deal.

i say. step back sisters. we're rising from the dead
i say. step back johnnies. we're dancing on our heads
i say. step back man. no mo hanging by a thread
i say. step back world. can't let it all go unsaid.

(2)

i say. all you young girls molested at ten
i say. all you young girls giving it up again & again
i say. all you sisters hanging out in every den
i say. all you sisters needing your own oxygen.

don't let them trap you with their coke
don't let them treat you like one fat joke
don't let them bleed you till you broke
don't let them blind you in masculine smoke.

i say, step back sisters. we're rising from the dead
i say. step back johnnies. we're dancing on our heads
i say. step back man. no mo hanging by a thread.
i say. step back world. can't let it go unsaid.

Response Poem

You Said
Marquesha Babers

It was something in the way you walked...
Something in the way you talked...
I mean you didn't quite give me butterflies
More like
Fireflies
Because every time you smiled I lit up.
But now every time I see your face,
I'm filled with disgust
And want to throw up.

All because August 16th, 2010...
That day I told you I liked you...
I just wanted to know if you liked me too.

I just wanted to know if you were feeling what I was feeling
    inside
But instead, I guess you thought it was a good day to make
    me cry
So you replied,
I must be stupid or out of my mind.

You said,
Maybe if I lost a little weight
But maybe not
Because I still can't change my face
You said I'll always look like this
And I'm not exactly model status.

I said,
You told me you would be there through any weather.
Now it's pouring and storming
And you just ran off with my umbrella.
You said I must have fallen and bumped my head
You said I must be dreaming.

I said,
Then why does this feel like a nightmare?
I'm not scared, just more hurt than anything.

You said,
It might be better if I died and came back reincarnated
　　as a beauty queen
Because right now I'm "not doing too good with this beauty
　　thing,"

So I said I would pray and wish that I were made of lead
So I could erase and start over like you said.
But I'm not
So instead I tried being dead.
You were the reason for my third suicide attempt
To come back different.

But I'm already different
So to come back from being different would mean to come
    back the same.
I said,
It's strange
I heard people say everyone's different

You said,
Stop
Stop making excuses to be useless.
You said the only reason people would be attracted to me is
Because of my breasts
And in the back of my mind I'm thinking,
Makes sense,
I mean
People have actually asked me my bra size
Before they asked me my name

So I said,
I'm going to start wearing hoodies to test this theory
To see if you couldn't see my chest how many people would
    come near me,
You said you would be willing to bet your whole life savings
    on "zero."
You said,
How many people do you know that want to be seen
Holding hands with the likes of you?
You said, "Zero."
I had a reply in the back of my mind...
But I stayed silent.

You didn't know it but I was trying to think of a way
To kill you and get away with it.
I wondered if I dipped your face in acid
How many of my pretty-face, hot-body friends would date
    you then...
I wanted to beat you until your own mother wouldn't be
    able to identify you
I wanted to show you what it felt like to be "zero."

Like you said
How many people do you know that want to be seen with the
    likes of you?
I WOULD BE WILLING TO BET "ZERO."

But killing you or disorienting your face seemed like a
    harsh way to go
So instead I said:
You are not nor will you ever be a real man
And you're scared that you can't handle me
So instead you talk down on me.
And you knew the extra pounds
Wasn't fat
It was love
And you could never measure up to what I deserve.

So I spit acid rain
In the form of words
To mess up your facial expression
And teach you a lesson.
Like I said
I'm different

And the more I try to change
The more I remain the same.

So you can front like I'm not everything you need and want.
But when the money is gone and so are the girls,
Don't try to come creeping back into my world,
Hiding behind bushes
Like I can't see your shadow
Because I like to go deep-sea diving,
And you're just
A little too...
Shallow.

Get Writing

Look in.

1. What's the hardest thing you've ever had to deal with?
2. When do you feel your childhood ended? Why? What happened?
3. Have you ever felt judged for how you look? How?
4. Is there a line from a song or story that means a lot to you? Why? What is it?
5. Do you take a lot of time to get close to people or do you get close too quickly? Why?

SHOUT out.

1. Is there anyone you've been having a conversation with in your head? Talk back to them in a poem.

2. Pick one line from Marquesha's poem "You Said" and use it to inspire a poem of your own.

Claim your classic.

Classic Poems about Love, Keeping an Open Heart, Being Fierce, Finding a Home, and Owning Your Worth

"A Certain Lady," Dorothy Parker

"How It Feels to Be Colored Me," Zora Neale Hurston

"I shall forget you presently, my dear," Edna St. Vincent Millay

"I Wrote a Good Omelet," Nikki Giovanni

"It Happens I Am a Singer of the Heart," Jimmy Santiago Baca

"One Wants a Teller In a Time Like This," Gwendolyn Brooks

"Phenomenal Woman," Maya Angelou

"Shapeshifter," Lucille Clifton

"This Is Not a Small Voice," Sonia Sanchez

"won't you celebrate with me," Lucille Clifton

WEARING DIFFERENT FACES
KHAMAL IWUANYANWU, IAN KOHN,
AND PATHUM MADIGAPOLA

"Wearing Different Faces" was written in response to "Ode to My Suit" by Pablo Neruda, a poem that reminded Khamal, Ian, and Pathum how people wake up every day and put on false personas to appease others. "Wearing Different Faces" was first performed at the Classic Slam.

P: Putting on this coat of happiness

K: It seems as if I am growing out of it

I: Happiness used to be who I was

All: But after falling down and being stepped on
      I realized that the coat was just too much

K: Too many patches

P: Too bright a shade

I: So I took off my coat

K: and put on my attitude

P: No more friendly hellos

I: No more laughter

K: But unless you keep a smile from ear to ear

All: The world will never accept you

I: People are allergic to hearing about depression.

P: My emotions can come off as offensive

All: So I gave up.

K: Put my attitude on the shelf

All: And walked around like nothing ever happened

I: Then I realized there was no difference between the
      sunshade I stood in and void.

All: This is not a story unique to us.

I: We are given just one body to live in yet we cannot seem
      to find a life to fit it.

I: The psychologist told me,

K: "If the environment doesn't change, you will implode."

I: I decided to hide depression under locks of hair covering
      my left eye.

P: My counselor said,

I: "Pathum, your teachers have been telling me that you haven't been happy in class. Is something wrong?"

I and K: "Can I do anything to help?"

P: No, let me just smile so that you don't become too concerned.

K: I told myself, If you don't start smiling again. Things will never get better. Grief doesn't bring back the dead.

All: Turn that frown upside down!

P: Get out of bed!

K: Turn off your music

I : Look at me when I'm talking to you

P: Why don't you smile anymore?

All: Turn that frown upside down

K: (I'm happy. I'm not sad anymore.)

I: I cover my entire face with a mask.

K: (I'm happy now.)

P: The mask that brings out the best in me

K: (I said I'm happy.)

I: I look for my mask before I step outside.

K: (I'm not sad anymore.)

P: I cower in my mask each time I talk to you.

K: (I'm happy.)

I: I reach for my mask whenever I look in the mirror

K: (I'm happy. I'm okay now.)

P: I depend on my mask whenever I want to be myself

K: (I said I'm happy. Stop asking me!)

I: In the wind

P: Through the night

K: (I'm happy!)

I: The streets and

P: the struggle

All: I swear to god I am happy!

    I SWEAR TO GOD I'M HAPPY!

    I SWEAR TO GOD—

I: We have a collection of masks lining our bedroom walls.

K: One for every situation.

    One for every location.

P: One for every person

All: I wonder which mask I'm going to wear for you.

11

JOCK

MATT BEYER, 18

Matt's Story

I enjoy spoken word for many of the same reasons I enjoy music—the mixture of language, rhythm, and expression. It reveals honesty unseen in everyday societal life. One of the purest satisfactions I know is hearing words that simultaneously rhyme and hold truth. I guess that's a joy that has always been in me, so maybe I was destined to write poetry. Still, I should probably acknowledge that in fourth grade, I wrote a horrendous poem that my teacher told me was amazing, and I believed her (which may have been why I first believed poetry was something I could do). Self-fulfilling prophecies will get you.

I don't consider myself a poet though. I mean, I write poetry, but I'm not a *poet*. I play baseball and guitar, but I don't really think of myself as an *athlete* or a *musician* either. I'm just *Matt-who-likes-to-do-things*. But my classmates only know one thing about me, it's usually that I play baseball. When I first joined the school spoken-word poetry team, I got the impression that a bunch of *poets* felt like an *athlete* was intruding upon their sacred space to express themselves. It was very uncomfortable for a short while, as I stereotyped the rest of the team, and they stereotyped me, and we all felt boxed in. Unfortunately, stereotyping comes naturally to pretty much everyone.

Luckily, I find that when people are open-minded, stereotypes quickly fade away, and it's easy to actually get to know people. That's what happened with my team, and I had a great experience with Harvard-Westlake spoken word. I felt like an equal member of the team, and I became friends with people whom I never would have without poetry. My experience on our team was unlike anything else I've experienced.

My English teacher read "One Art" by Elizabeth Bishop on the first day of school, and I was immediately drawn to it and its message: the realization that everything you ever have will eventually be lost. So when a girl didn't want to date me anymore, I thought back to the poem. I didn't feel shock from the loss because I had implicitly accepted that I would lose her just by having her at all (therein lies the inspiration for the first line of "Competitive Football"). From there, I created this weird, extended football metaphor. I used to play football (still not an *athlete*), and once I came up with one play on words related to the game, I thought I might be able to fill the whole poem with similar images. My poem was fun to write because it felt original. I could write forever if everything I came up with felt original, but things rarely do. I'm always wondering about the things my subconscious mind is plagiarizing. It's tiresome.

I intend to continue writing poetry in college, and I'll possibly attempt to join the spoken-word team at the school I'm attending. It's nice to decide what I do based on who I am, rather than the other way around.

Classic Poem

One Art
Elizabeth Bishop
The art of losing isn't hard to master;
so many things seem filled with the intent
to be lost that their loss is no disaster.

Lose something every day. Accept the fluster
of lost door keys, the hour badly spent.
The art of losing isn't hard to master.

Then practice losing farther, losing faster:
places, and names, and where it was you meant
to travel. None of these will bring disaster.

I lost my mother's watch. And look! my last, or
next-to-last, of three loved houses went.
The art of losing isn't hard to master.

I lost two cities, lovely ones. And, vaster,
some realms I owned, two rivers, a continent.
I miss them, but it wasn't a disaster.

—Even losing you (the joking voice, a gesture
I love) I shan't have lied. It's evident
the art of losing's not too hard to master
though it may look like (Write it!) like disaster.

Response Poem

Competitive Football
Matt Beyer

I knew—by having you—that I would have to lose you
But my selfish attitude hoped I would get to choose to.
Now I'm just a passing interference with a body that you
bruised through
Because I needed an anchor, and you just left the
newsroom.

We had highs minutes ago, but then you left the alma
mater
I knew you could hold me down, but then you kept me under
water
I know that I looked bubbly, but I wish that you looked
harder
I'm drowning in a bloodred sea; I'm not a very good parter.

I'm a false starter, I was jumping out with every sound you
made
That's a flag on the defensive team with no delay of
shame
That's a holding penalty; just let her go, it's just a game
Just give her two or three more days and she won't even
know your name.

—That's a hard hit for a loss of yards
A face mask up at school so no one sees your slew of scars
I never thought you'd get to me—I thought I had too many
guards

But there you were right off the blindside; now I'm seeing
    stars.

Well here's the red flag—I'm having all my plays reviewed
But I can't overturn my body full of days with you...
Next time you intercept a soul: announce it, if you're able
    to—
It isn't right to be a Steeler, and a Raider, too.

Get Writing

Look in.

1. Have you ever felt like you've had to pick one part of yourself over another?
2. What have you lost that's been hardest to lose?
3. When have you felt like the outsider?
4. What special skill do you have that would surprise other people?

SHOUT out.

1. Try copying writing elements of "Competitive Football," either by writing a sonnet with four stanzas of four lines, using end rhyme, or using metaphor as Matt has done with football as a metaphor for a relationship.
2. Write a poem about how you feel about losing things.
3. Write a letter to the thing that you've lost, explaining why you want it back.

Claim your classic.

Classic Poems on Letting Things Go

"A Very Short Song," Dorothy Parker

"Ah! Why, Because the Dazzling Sun," Emily Brontë

"How Poems Are Made, A Discredited View," Alice Walker

"If You Forget Me," Pablo Neruda

"*La Figlia Che Piange* (The Weeping Girl)," T. S. Eliot

"Letter to the Woman Who Stopped Writing Me Back," Jeffrey McDaniel

"Mad Girl's Love Song," Sylvia Plath

"Sonnet 147," William Shakespeare

"To Be In Love," Gwendolyn Brooks

"To have without holding," Marge Piercy

EMPTY

BELISSA ESCOBEDO, 15

Belissa's Story

My name is Belissa Escobedo, and I am a poet. It seems silly describing myself as a writer when even writing *this* gives me anxiety. There is always something to be grateful for and there is always something to mourn for. That idea is something that is, and probably always will be, hard for me to understand. To be able to still find the light when there's a complete blackout.

I love clichés. They are my thing. For me, the lights didn't go out all at once. It was during the span of one year—my sophomore year—that things started shutting down.

I have always been bullied. Unfortunately, that's a typical thing for young people to say nowadays. I was overweight since the day I could walk—my baby fat never seemed to melt away. I think that is one of the main reasons for my eating disorders. It also has to do with the fact that I, along with so many other girls my age, am heavily influenced by our society's pressure to be attractive and slim.

Luckily, my parents have been supportive. I appreciate them, but like any teenager and her parents, we have our disagreements. In my family, we share one trait and that's mental instability. We all seem to get along until one of us cracks and then the entire house comes crumbling down.

As hard as it is to write all of this down and try to show readers who I am or what I've become, these things have made me the person I am today. I'm ambitious, hard on myself (too much, most people would say), humorous (at least I like to think my puns are really funny), and loving. Really loving—I love everyone. Unless you're mean. This may not describe me down to the bone, but my poems do that for me. I'll keep writing them until I have a better way of telling you exactly who I am.

You can also tell a lot about a person by the poems they choose. I chose "Barbie Doll" by Marge Piercy because of its commentary on society's standards of beauty that are held over young women. The bluntness of the text and hollowness of the words carried on to my response poem, inspiring me to proceed in commenting on the harshness of society's morals.

For young teens reading this poem, remember what you are worth. Do not ever get caught up in the words of other people. They will tell you where to sit and live; and how to talk, walk, eat, speak, and be. But they are wrong. They'll never know who you are. Only you can decide where you will go next.

Classic Poem

Barbie Doll
Marge Piercy
This girlchild was born as usual
and presented dolls that did pee-pee
and miniature GE stoves and irons
and wee lipsticks the color of cherry candy.
Then in the magic of puberty, a classmate said:
You have a great big nose and fat legs.

She was healthy, tested intelligent,
possessed strong arms and back,
abundant sexual drive and manual dexterity.
She went to and fro apologizing.
Everyone saw a fat nose on thick legs.

She was advised to play coy,
exhorted to come on hearty,
exercise, diet, smile and wheedle.
Her good nature wore out
like a fan belt.
So she cut off her nose and her legs
and offered them up.

In the casket displayed on satin she lay
with the undertaker's cosmetics painted on,
a turned-up putty nose,
dressed in a pink and white nightie.
Doesn't she look pretty? everyone said.
Consummation at last.
To every woman a happy ending.

Response Poem

ED
Belissa Escobedo

There's something attractive about food.
The way it slithers down your throat, hot or cold
into the acid pool in your bloated stomach waiting to
    further digest it.
Our body's digestive system is made up of hollow organs
yet we choose to fill them daily.
Every minute of the day there is an urge
to suck up every ounce of fat lying in front of you
besides the lard that is hanging from your own body.
An average person's stomach is the size of their two fists
    placed next to each other. Now either I have the
    hands of a full-grown Ape
or I was just blessed with an abnormally large,
disproportionate, muscular sac.
Tell me, why is it that every time I go to a restaurant
I spend fifteen minutes arguing with myself over what I
    should get
calculating my caloric intake
adding and subtracting the worth of each crumb
praising myself for at least comprehending basic math
I have to remind myself that you cannot fill those hollow
    organs
without them filling you.
Without making every person, pity in their eyes,
stare at the poor obese girl crying over spilled milk.
I can't forget what is important.
What it was like.

11 years old and told by the love of my life
through a Facebook message
"don't wear short skirts anymore stupid
u aren't skinny don't forget that stupid
and close ur legs when u sit down disgusting"
I have to give him some credit.
Without him I would've never woken up and finally accepted
    the fact that I was fat and no one would ever love me
because I was too, too much to carry.
I had to learn to carry myself.
All of the weight on my back, at first it was hard
but it became a challenge I had to accept.
It was leaving my path of 500 calories or less
because I'd already been told countless times
it takes 1200 for the heart to fully function.
I refused to watch myself disappear.
My bones looked nice protruding even when people started
    asking if I was sick.
I wanted to feel beautiful and even then, at my lowest
    and smallest
I still felt like my body could never be seen next to my
    beautiful friends and models.
The public eye had to be kept away.
I've been kept away for a long time
and I've been afraid of saying this out loud
because I don't want anyone to hear my words
and think I agree with what I do.
I realize that it is wrong to restrict yourself to the point of
    sickness.
Curled into a tight ball the pain can't pass off as cramps.
You haven't had your period in 5 months.

You're becoming a walking waste.
You've damaged every cell in your body.
You are weak.
That's where the doctors got it wrong.
I will never be weak.
I get up each day, force myself to look in the mirror
crack a smile even
that way I can see what I've been missing.
There is beauty in me and I haven't found it yet
but when I do I'll know that every meal I turned down,
every scream I muffled in the dressing rooms,
every calorie I counted
will not have made me weak.
It will have made me who I am today
not broken
not romanticized
not crying for help
not just a disorder.

I will be beautiful.

Get Writing

Look in.

1. What are you grateful for? What do you mourn for?
2. How do you love? Fiercely? Tentatively? Wholeheartedly?
3. Is there a way that you abuse yourself?
4. What is your relationship to your body like?
5. What do others judge you for? How do you handle it?

SHOUT out.

1. Write about the ways you've had to "learn to carry" yourself.
2. Write a poem about being seen. Do you feel seen? By which people?
   Who do you wish saw you that doesn't?

Claim your classic.

**Classic Poems about Body Image, Identity, Cultivating Worthiness
from the Inside Out, and Dying While We Live**

"Instructions for a Body," Marty McConnell

"Living in the Body," Joyce Sutphen

"Mirror," Sylvia Plath

"Monologue of a Broadway Actress," Yevgeny Yevtushenko

"Now," Audre Lorde

"She Had Some Horses," Joy Harjo

"Snapping Beans," Lisa Parker

"The Applicant," Sylvia Plath

"Weighing In," Rhina Espaillat

"Wild Geese," Mary Oliver

13

CRUNCHY

MIRIAM SACHS, 16

Miriam's Story

I began on November 30 at 9:11 PM. I don't remember this. It was told to me afterward, slowly, like sipping a thick milkshake through a thin straw. I grew up slowly as well, or grew into my brain, or planted a brain to begin with. I am just another human being created from ancient stardust and shaped into something impossible that nobody can explain. I was born and my life started at that second, like a line stemming from a fixed point. I don't remember it, but I have pictures I could show you if you ask.

My parents tell me I did lots of things when I was little. I could talk at an early age. I climbed trees. I also ate the sand every time we went to the beach. (We stopped going to the beach.) As I got older, the memories faded up to somewhere recognizable, and I can almost pretend that the child was me. I played basketball and cut my hair short. I liked Power

Rangers, tag, and playing pretend with stuffed animals and a broken drum set. I always loved stories.

In the summer before fourth grade, I acted in my first play, *Peter Pan*, and played the complex role of Curly the Lost Boy. I never stopped performing. Since then, I've been in twenty-plus productions with various theater companies. Now I work as student staff for Encore Entertainers, teaching kids who reflect my own past right back at me like compact mirrors with jazz shoes and horrible singing voices.

In fifth grade, I wrote an entire novel in a composition book. It was green and college ruled, and I wrote the novel in all different colors. One day, my teacher caught me writing during science and told me to see him after class. He pulled out a worn paperback and placed it in my hands, telling me it was his college textbook for creative writing. Ever since then, *Writing Down the Bones* has guided me into the universe of words and language that is so existential and raw it can't be described with words and language. The book talked about writing as a way of life, so I started journaling and crafting stories and poetry. This helped me escape life and delve deeper into it at the same time. It became my lifeline and my inspiration to keep building myself up like an endless elevator into somewhere nobody has ever been before and someplace I want to go.

The funny thing about going in the generally accepted direction of forward with your life is that you tend to stumble into things on the way. Sometimes you hit a pole and it really hurts your head. Other times you find things like poetry and lifelong friends. It makes me think about how everything is so completely chaotic, and yet, I have ended up here.

Last year, I went to the *LA Times* Festival of Books and saw the booth for Get Lit. I picked up a flyer for the Classic Slam, but I didn't understand. I thought my school had to be affiliated with the program in order for me to attend, and it wasn't. Then, six months later, I won a Poetry Out Loud competition at my school and went on to compete at the county level. After performing, I met two teachers who told me I should join Get Lit. They explained that I could come to the Saturday class even if my school didn't know the organization. So through the puppet strings that the universe pulls in its playtime, I ended up spitting slam poetry and discovering something that resembles a passion.

The classic poem "Touched by an Angel" shows me that even though sometimes falling in love or getting really passionate about something can have its downfalls and drive you a little bit crazy, it is still worth it to keep loving and feeling because it sets you free. When there's something that you love a lot or that you give all of yourself to, it can be difficult and rewarding. I like how the poem gives all sides of love and also ends on the idea that it is worth it. I also think it can apply not just to people, as in romantic love, but to things like writing or family or poetry.

My response is more specifically related to the romantic aspect of love, but it also does not see love as a one-dimensional thing. My response presents passion from its many angles, showing that it's not all good or all bad, but more complex than that.

In closing, I guess my life story is everything that has led up to my existence right now. Looking back on the past, it sounds like the events were planned out or predetermined—as if, somehow, where I am is where I need to be; as if, somehow, it's all going to turn out right. Writing helps me to be aware, to focus on the world and think about it, to look up from my pinpoint perspective and branch out into the roots of what it really means to be a hungry Homo sapiens. We are all lost and toppling over our own values like animals searching for a savior. And I don't think the journey is ever complete; I think it's the process itself that counts.

And that's what writing is about. After you finish a piece, you don't stop. You keep questioning the mystery that is everyday existence. You keep digging with a pen for a shovel. You keep searching and searching to explain and understand the beautiful catastrophe circling like a snowstorm around us. You keep writing.

Classic Poem

Touched by an Angel
Maya Angelou
We, unaccustomed to courage
exiles from delight
live coiled in shells of loneliness
until love leaves its high holy temple
and comes into our sight
to liberate us into life.

Love arrives
and in its train come ecstasies
old memories of pleasure
ancient histories of pain.
Yet if we are bold,
love strikes away the chains of fear
from our souls.

We are weaned from our timidity
In the flush of love's light
we dare be brave
And suddenly we see
that love costs all we are
and will ever be.
Yet it is only love
which sets us free.

Response Poem

Reckless Union
Miriam Sachs

I watch you. I wonder if you are aware.
I'm crazed with spinning,
feeling like a drunk evaporation
split-second stopped, suddenly swooping,
shell-shocked.
I want to be beautiful.
Not just for you, but independently for me;
to be admired from a severed standpoint,
the way you are.
And wanting separation from a sorrow tied to childhood
chirping in the back of my mind,
a past I can't rewind but would rather record over and
　　　leave behind.
I move forward, unlock my car door, adjust the mirrors,
and drive across a fantasy that slides
into a silver streamline that might just be mine.

It begins and ends,
the life reminds the liver to look around.
It gets dangerous to stay alone in one room with myself
for multiple, mannered moments.
I'm a byproduct of this wet new love I wish I could rock.
But how do I talk to you?
It's the romance movement in cinema.
I want to stretch its sins around me and open up
another door I've never breathed about before.
But it's still mine,

that faraway planet made of granite,
backward lessons,
and my recession's deep depression.
Let's discover love together.

I'll be wandering.
You can find me hanging out with Cool.
You can kiss me if you do,
but if you don't I'll bury my body
and board this eschew transition to a plane
that worries whether its wings are feign or true.
I'm soaring in the stain that desires a timeless nighttime,
losing Right and finding You.
I have two eyes for looking lonely
and insecurities scarring my certainty
but somehow you and I will walk like gravity in another
     masterpiece.
We'll talk like the dialogue should be written down,
I'm ready for your eyes,
they are the expanding direction of the universe.
I'll take you out to lunch somewhere no one's been.
Because this is the feeling I wake up in the morning for.
You are the iconic image of valuable adolescence
that lingers like a raincloud when the body's sick with
     drought.
I want the soft hair, dry hands, silent snare.
I want your delicate demeanor,
meant for only me to see her,
we to free her,
us to be.

Only you don't see me.
My skin is liquid invisible.
I worry I'm inventing the connection,
but it's the only one that's worth it.
Mine, ours, us, this secret sound existence,
this excruciating darkness,
this blue dream of reckless union.

Get Writing

Look in.

1. What are the things you used to do but don't any longer? Why not?
2. What are you most proud of?
3. Is there someone that you're crazy in love with?
4. What makes someone fulfill the requirements of being a lifelong friend?
5. Do you think your life is predestined? What makes you think that?

SHOUT out.

1. Write about what your life would look like if it were a landscape painting. Would it be a desert? A beach? An open field? Who would you want to go there with? Be there with that person now.
2. Write a poem about the most important lesson you've ever learned. How did your life change by learning it?

Claim your classic.

Poems about Loving, Growing Up, and Discovering Passion

"Axis," Octavio Paz

"Desire," Alice Walker

"Love's Philosophy," Percy Bysshe Shelley

"Song Out Here," Juan Felipe Herrera

"Song," Allen Ginsberg

"Sonnets from the Portuguese 43," Elizabeth Barrett Browning

"The Archipelago of Kisses," Jeffrey McDaniel

"the great advantage of being alive," E. E. Cummings

"The Secret," Jeffrey McDaniel

"When You Are Old," William Butler Yeats

14

BLACK BOY
KHAMAL IWUANYANWU, 16

Khamal's Story

My ideology is mostly based on the sayings of my elders. My grandfather encapsulated my entire mind-set in one phrase: "Wear your heart on your sleeve and keep everyone else's on your mind." That's how I've always wanted to lead my life: strong, smart, resourceful, and most important, compassionate enough to help everyone I encounter. Through my struggle and strife, this mind-set keeps me sane and hopeful.

Compassion. I value this more than any other human quality. It brings about empathy, peace, and joy, yet it is almost extinct everywhere I look. In fact, my very existence seems to attract the exact opposite: hate.

Being a black boy, I was exposed to racism, discrimination, and hatred at a very young age. Born and raised in Southern California, I was one of

five or six black people in my entire elementary school, and my neighborhood was mostly Hispanic. In first grade, I heard my first racial slur. A
classmate called me a "nigger"; I didn't know what it meant, but I knew
it was derogatory by the way he spat it out at me—as though he couldn't
bear the taste of it in his mouth. I did not tell anyone because I felt it was
just a run-of-the-mill, mean-spirited insult of a peer.

But that word became a recurring theme in my life. In fifth grade,
I learned about slavery and, specifically, the origins of the word "nigger." My first thought was to laugh because my grandma was white and
my dad was born in Nigeria. But the idea of slavery haunted me. Eventually, I realized that slavery wasn't what I should be concerned about.
Discrimination seemed more frequent, or at least I noticed it more
often. Previously normal days became more sinister. I became hyper-
aware of the divide between my peers and I, and I could see no reason
other than race.

It began with my peers, then extended to family members. The
European side of my family separated themselves from my black family
at every possible opportunity. Family reunions became empty conversations with a couple relatives and Christmas grew lonelier every year.
As a young black boy, I felt a circle of hatred beginning to narrow in
on me.

Grief sunk into my being and became a part of who I was. I became
aware of a condition I call "black boy"—a label that has been placed on
me in many aspects of life. I can never be just a boy—"black" is a prefix
that most people deem necessary to add in front. And by being a boy
with dark skin—a black boy—I have to deal with racially motivated discrimination, violence, and just flat-out hatred from people as close as my
own family members to those far removed, such as a random passerby
I may, by chance, encounter on the street. That's what it means to be a
black boy.

It seemed that every single person found it necessary to give me
advice about this condition: "You're black. Get used to gang violence."

"Black people are so emotional." I selected this classic poem by Sekou Sundiata because of the ways it connects to me and all the other black boys. Although I uphold the law, I have had multiple confrontations and frightening incidents with the enforcers of the law. I've seen close friends be physically subdued while being completely docile, and I have been followed and questioned by police simply because of my skin color.

I *am* a black boy, but I am not *just* a black boy. I am a gold medalist in the academic decathlon, an expert in free running, a poet, and a state-certified gifted student. I am much more than just my skin. I am not confined to my color. I come from a family of artists and scientists. My skin does not belie my soul. I am as black as black can be. I am Langston Hughes, the Harlem renaissance, Barack Obama, leader of the free-world black. I am the nations, cultures, music, and art all across the world black. I am a black boy and I accept that because it means that I have a history of forgotten greatness that I need only to exhume from the earth.

I became a writer to show myself and everyone like me that we can amount to something. We can aspire to be something greater than a statistic. My world is not gang signs; it is poetry.

I became a writer to substantiate this idea, and after a lot of work, I became the highest-scoring poet of the 2015 Get Lit Classic Slam. I have multiple works published in literary magazines. And most important, I've been able to share what I have to say with many, many people.

Beyond poetry, I give my compassion to people I encounter. I volunteer at the polls, I give blood, I tutor, and I have personally saved ten people. I saved these people in different ways: some were drowning, and some were injured and I carried them to safety. I taught three grown men how to swim, and they went on to become marines.

I am so much more than just my skin. I am my compassion. I am my actions. And those are golden.

Classic Poem

Blink Your Eyes
Sekou Sundiata
(Remembering Sterling A. Brown)
I was on my way to see my woman
but the Law said I was on my way
thru a red light red light red light
and if you saw my woman
you could understand,
I was just being a man.
It wasn't about no light
it was about my ride
and if you saw my ride
you could dig that too, you dig?
Sunroof stereo radio black leather
bucket seats sit low you know,
the body's cool, but the tires are worn.
Ride when the hard time come, ride
when they're gone, in other words
the light was green.

I could wake up in the morning
without a warning
and my world could change:
blink your eyes.
All depends, all depends on the skin,
all depends on the skin you're living in

Up to the window comes the Law
with his hand on his gun

what's up? what's happening?
I said I guess
that's when I really broke the law.
He said a routine, step out the car
a routine, assume the position.
Put your hands up in the air
you know the routine, like you just don't care.
License and registration.
Deep was the night and the light
from the North Star on the car door, déjà vu
we've been through this before,
why did you stop me?
Somebody had to stop you.
I watch the news, you always lose.
You're unreliable, that's undeniable.
This is serious, you could be dangerous.

I could wake up in the morning
without a warning
and my world could change:
blink your eyes.
All depends, all depends on the skin,
all depends on the skin you're living in
New York City, they got laws
can't no bruthas drive outdoors,
in certain neighborhoods, on particular streets
near and around certain types of people.
They got laws.
All depends, all depends on the skin,
all depends on the skin you're living in.

Response Poem

Sepia
Khamal Iwuanyanwu

Autumn leaves fall from aging trees,
the sun rays leave the air in a golden haze,
hey there, hello.
I never realized how beautiful the sky could be yellow.
Almost as beautiful as a deep black night,
lit up only by the distant glinting good-byes of stars millions
    of light-years away.
But I can't enjoy that today.
Or tonight,
or any other time I exist
because if you have too much melanin in your skin,
people don't accept you under the sun,
and at night you must stay in.
I am a black boy.
I cannot go to Starbucks without getting shady looks from
    baristas and customers,
who feel that I'm trying to act white by ordering a chai
    cream frap with blend the whip,
no cinnamon and 3 heavy-handed pumps of chai.
Better make that with soy milk
because I'm lactose intolerant.
I cannot stomach the white of your milk
just to make the black of my coffee more appetizing.
Easier for your palette to accept, easier for your stomach
    to digest.
I'd rather let my words sit there.

Let them fester in your gut where then maybe, just maybe,
    they might be heard.

This is not my story. This is our story.
The story of the black boy.
Black boy!
Be proud of your skin! It is not a scar but a medal of honor,
a trophy carried down by each and every one of your kin.
Black boy!
Beware of your skin! It is not a trophy, but a target, a mark
    for the bullet to hit!
Black boy!
We are all human! It is your heart that matters,
don't worry about the color of your skin.
But I have to because I am a black boy!
Please do not tell me that I'm not, because I know I am.
A black boy will try his best to act right,
in hopes that they might mistake him for white.
Black boy!
Don't you dare wear a black hoodie at night, black boy,
no matter how much you want to fade into the night.
Paint your skin with the chalk in your class and they might
    forget what you are,
a black boy,
but don't take it too far black boy!
Or you might end up another dead black boy.
We don't need any more dead black boys.
So bring him to me,
Bring me the black boy!
Which one?
The smart one!

Which one?
The strong one!
Which one?!
My name is Khamal
I am not just a black boy,
I am not the chains cuffed around your wrists.
I am not a noose hooked around your neck.
I am not a burning cross on your front yard.
So why do you hate me?
My only offense was being born darker than you.

Get Writing

Look in.

1. Is there any kind of division in your family?
2. How do you straddle that divide? Or do you heal it?
3. Have you ever felt judged for the color of your skin?
4. What is your response to racism?
5. What are the things that you are most proud of?

SHOUT out.

1. Write a poem starting every line with the words "I Am," listing all of the things that comprise who you are.
2. Write a poem to the lawmakers in this country. What would you like them to know?

Claim your classic.

Classic Poems about Color, Race, and Equality

"Anthem for Doomed Youth," Wilfred Owen

"Black History," Gil Scott-Heron

"Dream Variations," Langston Hughes

"If We Must Die," Claude McKay

"Incident," Countee Cullen

"Ka'Ba," Amiri Baraka

"No Difference," Shel Silverstein

"Race," Elizabeth Alexander

"The Times," Lucille Clifton

"Wake Me When I'm Free," Tupac Shakur

> We are the universe contemplating itself.
>
> **—Carl Sagan**

RAVER

RYAN JAFAR, 22

Ryan's Story

I feel like I embody the clichéd notion of a tormented genius. But what fool would even have the audacity to label himself *a genius?* Ha-ha! I don't know; that's just how I feel, and I'm trying to be honest. I'm the kind of fool in constant war with my ego—to the point that I have gone through periods of time completely forgetting how to even act like my own self, stricken by depression from overanalyzing the space between uttered words in conversations and, consequentially, losing my own frame of sociability, forgetting how to laugh normally in response to someone's joke, and being obsessed over whether the eye contact in a particular situation was one nanosecond too long.

This was me when I started college (but not anymore, so hold back that intervention you were planning!). This was my reaction to an intentional decision I made to party excessively my first year and extend the limits of my usual consciousness.

It made me the polar opposite of the Ryan in high school who was ambitious, dream driven, focused to obsession on goals, and extremely social/confident (I mean in general, obviously). Yes, that same Ryan, who was a rhyme fanatic, MC at heart without any developed interest in poetry; who, on some off-chance teacher recommendation to try out for some random spoken-word thingamajig because it said "performances throughout LA," ended up becoming the initial Get Lit troupe that catapulted him into the ranks of the top-ten international poets, and who pushed his skill-set as a writer/performer multiple galaxies beyond that of a mere lyrical rapper.

Then, in my first years of college, I dissipated into a cove that could only echo a shell of who I once was. The truth is, I sort of let myself BECOME this bleak mind-set; it was an actual semiconscious/subconscious decision, I think. In my mind, this was a path of life I wanted to walk and understand for no other reason than my own curiosity to view things through a lens other than my own. As a result, when at my worst, I lost my passion, my creativity was cast into the darkest oceans, and I almost gave up on my aspirations for the entertainment career I'd always sought.

Two things I learned from this state: (1) my introspective world is just as large as the outside reality beyond the looking glass; and (2) there would be no boundaries, limitations, or uncharted territory on my quest to create art.

Beyond the looking glass is reality. Both my parents emigrated from a third-world nation and paid the price with all the sacrifice and hard work that go into such a decision. As a child, I always had trouble fitting in, which resulted in a heavy rotation of me getting picked on every year until high school. Although I feel it was brought on by the fact that my mother dressed me like a Bangladeshi student (aka FOB, or fresh off the boat— ha-ha!), it was most likely a significant factor in shaping the way I turned out. The inability to fit in led me to the arts, and I drifted through the roads of comic-book art, drawing, story writing, and acting to eventually end up in music (specifically as an MC/rapper).

Rather than try to explain this arrival, I can simply say that when I began to write rap lyrics, everything just clicked. Then the next thing I knew, I was dedicating myself to becoming the best lyricist on the planet! I was so obsessed that I began reading college-level novels and *the dictionary* on my high school bus, because I realized this time would just be wasted by napping. Instead, if I forced myself to read something I might not otherwise, I could gain vocabulary skills to help further my rapping abilities. (LOL—what am I, a computer?)

Then came the introduction to the underground LA rap scene— Project Blowed—and Diane with her spoken word, and the rest became history!

I still haven't really described the story of my life. I suppose I don't fully understand it yet. The best I can do is describe the events up to when I became this person who is typing right now. In my mind, my story is still just beginning. But the one crucial fact I've understood from all this nonsensical gibberish is that I am completely and utterly dedicated to exploring the outlet of art to its maximum peak.

Like the quote in the beginning, I am "itself" attempting to understand "itself." I am far too young to tell you about my life, and much too confused and foolish to give explanations for so broad a topic. I am the beginning segment of my life attempting to contemplate its own entirety. All I know is this: art makes sense, and it has always made sense. It's the only thing that ever makes sense. When I sit down to create, regardless of the medium, I flourish. I don't know why, but I was born to be an artist.

I periodically recall a fragment from *Faust* that I memorized in Get Lit years back: "I want frenzied excitements, gratifications that are painful, love and hatred violently mixed, anguish that enlivens, inspiriting trouble." It is about experiencing all facets of human emotion and not as simplistic ideas of happy and sad. The writer wants frenzied excitements, not just excitement by itself! Emotions contradict, overlap, and, for an artist, are golden treasure chests.

In the following poem that I wrote as a response to Longfellow, you will notice I do not rhyme at all; in fact, I did not display a single root of my hip-hop background when I wrote this poem. I explored the medium of poetry for what it is and expressed a part of myself that could not properly be done otherwise. Therefore, I feel my poem answers Longfellow's, as they both explore the concept of reciprocating unconditional love. Longfellow's poem "The Children's Hour" is a magical journey into a child's magnificent imagination set alive by a warm-hearted father who experiences utter joy from his children's playful nature. The poem I wrote, "My Turn," is a perfect response to this fatherly lens of adoration for children. The subject explores my strong desire to reciprocate that unconditional love my father gave to me. It also offers a contrasting lens that shows the sacrifices a father might make for the same children he so openly loves. And once the child becomes an adult, they begin to understand that our warm fathers were actually much, much more than that "fortress" to "scale over" and topple.

Every occupation has a purpose; a cop is supposed to uphold the law, and an architect is supposed to outline structural designs. To me, an artist is supposed to explore human emotion in every possible facet without prejudice, bias, or even self-preservation. And that is what I am going to do: be a crazy, tormented, completely happy, glorious Artist. You can toss me in the dungeons or shower me with riches, but I will never stop exploring the tunnels of self-expression.

Classic Poem

The Children's Hour
Henry Wadsworth Longfellow
Between the dark and the daylight,
        When the night is beginning to lower,
Comes a pause in the day's occupations,
        That is known as the Children's Hour.

I hear in the chamber above me
        The patter of little feet,
The sound of a door that is opened,
        And voices soft and sweet.

From my study I see in the lamplight,
        Descending the broad hall stair,
Grave Alice, and laughing Allegra,
        And Edith with golden hair.

A whisper, and then a silence:
        Yet I know by their merry eyes
They are plotting and planning together
        To take me by surprise.

A sudden rush from the stairway,
        A sudden raid from the hall!
By three doors left unguarded
        They enter my castle wall!

They climb up into my turret
        O'er the arms and back of my chair;

If I try to escape, they surround me;
    They seem to be everywhere.

They almost devour me with kisses,
    Their arms about me entwine,
Till I think of the Bishop of Bingen
    In his Mouse-Tower on the Rhine!

Do you think, O blue-eyed banditti,
    Because you have scaled the wall,
Such an old mustache as I am
    Is not a match for you all!

I have you fast in my fortress,
    And will not let you depart,
But put you down into the dungeon
    In the round-tower of my heart.

And there will I keep you forever,
    Yes, forever and a day,
Till the walls shall crumble to ruin,
    And moulder in dust away!

Response Poem

My Turn
Ryan Jafar

Your eyes weld yellow
like the backs of palms of immigrant hands,
Burnt from the sun's wet lips,

I wonder how men
can work like machines
but behave like love,

It seems reality is our worst enemy
because it proves nothing is deserved,
For if such a state existed
you would be elected governor,
I only hope to carry you
as you have carried me from the newborn ripe for picking,
And if the fruits you bear from labor
diminish from the world's cruelty,
I will harvest you a thousand farms over,

Your eyes assemble imprints of the cold hands from stress
but a kindness that even the universe is not ready to
    understand,
I stand indifferent,
but hide the tears from your pain,
I only hope to give you sunlight,
The kind that dazzles like shimmering crystals at the
    crack of dawn,
because you deserve it,
But the universe is apathetic
and you are passion,
the kind bottled up in a small boy of dreams,
me,
I want to free you from your chains
and let your eyes soar like the eagles they are,
You are my father,
My motivation,

My candle of light eluding the whispering winds of the
    world,
I only hope to give you happiness,
For all the fame and wealth I attain
will all be for you,
Just give me your feet on a couch,
and your mind on a beach
to swim into your dreams
because it is my turn...
to work.

Get Writing

Look in.

1. What do you want to achieve?
2. Do you ever second-guess things you've said? Play over the dialogue in your head.
3. Are there two sides of you in conflict? (For example, introvert versus extrovert.) Write about the two sides.
4. What feels like the most authentic form of artistic expression for you?
5. How do your parents' sacrifices spur you on to succeed?

SHOUT out.

1. Write a poem about an unexplored feeling.
2. Rewrite a conversation you keep replaying in your head. Make it into art.

3. Write out a dialogue between the two sides of yourself. They can become two characters in story. They can alternate writing each line of a poem.

Claim your classic.

Classic Poems about Understanding Inner Depths, Making Great Art, Seeking Success, and Honoring the Sacrifices of Our Ancestors

"Age of Consent," Lenore Kandel

"Faust, Parts I and II," Johann Wolfgang von Goethe

"Fury," Lucille Clifton

"Howl," Allen Ginsberg

"Instructions to a Poet Who Suspects His Own Mediocrity," Patricia Smith

"Me! Come! My Dazzled Face," Emily Dickinson

"On Reason and Passion," Kahlil Gibran

"Success," Ralph Waldo Emerson

"Those Winter Sundays," Robert Hayden

"Your Beautiful Parched, Holy Mouth," Hafiz

MISFIT
EMILY JAMES, 17

Emily's Story

My uncle once told me that when I was born, I was dealt a hand with no winning cards. He believed this because I'm a girl, I'm Hispanic, and I'm the daughter of a father who's been in prison for a majority of both our lives. How could anyone be pleased with those odds?

Being a girl was never actually a burden to me. I was lucky enough to have grandparents and a mother who allowed me to explore more than just the "normal" girlish activities. From books to soccer to Texas Hold'em, there were no boundaries, and I loved every minute of it.

Instead, the real burden was coming to the realization that I am not only a girl but a lesbian girl, to be exact. I grew up with my grandmother who dreamed of the day I would walk down an aisle and spend the rest of my life with a man. I grew up with my grandfather who initially believed it was his fault I strayed from the straight path. Worst of all, though, I grew up with my mother who still loved me (and claims to have always known I had a fondness for the ladies) but was, nonetheless, scared for what the real world could potentially thrust upon me: hate crimes, abuse, and just plain negativity.

She was right. Teasing led to slurs, which led to arguments, which eventually led to a few black eyes and a couple of scars. Now I just think of them as interesting stories to tell. There were times in my home when arguments would simmer in the form of complete silence throughout the house. I felt as if my family truly wished they could change me—not because they didn't love me but because they loved me so much they didn't want me to have to go through more pain than I would already have to just by being human.

The second unlucky card was being Hispanic. My last name is James, probably the "whitest name ever," and I have a complexion that resembles snow, so it's always hard for people to believe that my mother was born and raised in El Salvador for the first ten years of her life. I will admit my uncle was half-right: being Hispanic was pretty hard some-times, but not in the way he thought. It's hard being Hispanic and living in a primarily Hispanic neighborhood when no one believes I'm actually Hispanic. I can never really enter a conversation about how great it is to eat *pupusas* with *chicharrón* and *plátanos* when my last name reminds people of a lot of historical figures in US history.

The worst part about the whole scenario is that it essentially made me feel like a hybrid. I was never dark enough to be fully accepted as more than the "white girl" in school, but I was always too ethnic to hang out comfortably with white kids. Many people may look at this and say I should be grateful for the fact that I have "white privilege," but the reality is this: if I could give it away, I would.

The third and most unlucky card (in the opinion of my uncle) was growing up without a father. I would be lying if I said it never bothered me. Growing up without a dad to take me to soccer games, teach me to drive, or even ground me was never something I enjoyed. In fact, it was something I loathed. I started fights with anyone who tried to talk to me about my dad. I destroyed a friendship because a girl offered to "share her dad." Looking back, she was just being kind, and I was being obnoxious. Today, not having a father around just seems normal. Seeing my friends with their dads is the real taboo for me.

I don't know if my outlook on fathers changed drastically because I allowed myself to swallow up my sadness after my father left me alone at a party for hours to go buy beer and get high. But I do recognize that my father did teach me things. He taught me what abandonment feels like, but more importantly, he taught me how to grow up and face those feelings of abandonment and, essentially, kick them in the groin. I know how to handle loneliness, and I know how to be strong even when it seems like everything around me resembles the destruction after a massive hurricane.

In essence, my uncle was right—my cards were stacked against me. With what I was dealt, most people would assume I'd do very little. However, in English class, I learned that many Greek philosophers agreed that a person doesn't have true wisdom until they've encountered pain. My cards at birth were horrible, but I can say that's why I am so genuinely happy now. All these bad cards just made me want to fight for the good ones.

So I did.

I started appreciating *people* more instead of appreciating things. I started finding even the smallest reasons to smile. Even if there were days when absolutely nothing was right, sometimes I would fake happiness. I'd fake it until I believed it, and at that point when I believed it, I wasn't faking it anymore. Now I have grandparents who are proud that I've been accepted to college, a mother who is proud to say I take her lessons seriously, friends who couldn't care less that I'm a snowflake in Southern California, and a girlfriend who makes sure I love myself before I love anyone else. Having all of this makes me hope that I always receive the worst cards, so I can fight to make them better.

I always loved Biggie Smalls, and my entire junior year of high school was dedicated to listening to "Things Done Changed." So when Francisco X. Alarcón's piece "Memorial" appeared, I felt a connection between Alarcón's story of a saddened city and Biggie's story of a changed city. My response poem answers Alarcón's piece by creating a city that was run-down in almost every way. The city I grew up in luckily does not resemble this horrendous life anymore, but at one point in my life, it did. My friends and I still remember how our city used to be. A lot of those memories we don't wish to share, but our actions to push ourselves to get out of this city speak for themselves.

I heard once that sharing a story can be therapeutic, so I wanted my response to be therapeutic. Which is why I created the hopeful ending, and I honestly couldn't think of anyone more hopeful or wise than my mother. So it was natural that I turn her into a giant metaphor.

Classic Poem

Memorial
Francisco X. Alarcón
The Pacific Garden Mall as we know it
ceased to exist at 5:04 today.—Mardi Wormhoudt,
Mayor of Santa Cruz, October 17, 1989

do towns
suffer
like people
heart attacks

do buildings
get scared
too and try
to run

do steel
frames
get twisted
out of pain

do windows
break
because
they can't cry

do walls let
themselves go
just
like that

and lie on
sidewalks
waiting
to be revived

is this how
old places
give birth
to new places?

Response Poem

Momma
Emily James

My town was my momma! Always good to me...
But suddenly the simple me
grew up and found out my street and a couple blocks down
didn't count as the "whole town."
You could smell the sickness from miles around.
My friends making new decisions about
whether the disease of drive-bys, dropouts,
or drug busts would take them out.
This town had been suffering years of strife...
Momma crouched over and clutched her heart for dear
    life
Because my friends were outta their minds! Dopin' up and
    gettin' high!
Becoming fiends and watching their lives float by
With every new breath of that buddha
Or hit of that steppin-stone drug, hookah.

Momma wept in pain

Knowing this neighborhood might die in vain.

As the streets carried on

Her alleyways feared their fight wouldn't be won

Feared for the people who wouldn't live to see dawn

These people, these kids, my friends, Shawn.

My momma feared for Shawn.

He sat watching her walls crack in his mind

Hoping he could find beauty intertwined

Within the tainted pieces.

Knowing if he could hold beauty

He could hold sanity.

If her buildings could leave they would...instead they
    found Shawn's body inside

With no passion. No fire in his eyes.

The boy who wished to go gently into that good night

found his father's gun—decided he was done

clutched it even though he was too young

And screamed good-bye!

One hand held a gun.

The other was bloodied from picking too hard at the
    plaster—his life hadn't even begun.

But the buildings weren't the only ones who felt insane...

No—her windows also felt a presence of pain

They witnessed me, the silent arguments in my head

Of how to leave this town before I'm dead.

Pacing the room until the floor became thin and the holes
    in my shoes

Became another way to show my heart's wounds.

From years of anger toward my friends because they
    betrayed my town, my Momma.

They witnessed the daydreaming kids who knew there
    was a slim chance
Of not having to dance
With death before they were 18.
When her windows shattered, Momma knew the next scene:
Some kid so angry that crying wasn't the only thing he
    could do
He had to see something smash apart to feel something
    close to true.
And my town, my Momma, saw her children breakin'
Each child, each friend, taken
By a disease of his choice: drive-bys, dropouts, or drug
    busts
Until he could only be kept together by a chain and two
    cuffs.
As silver as the steel cage where he'd wind up.
All this pain began chipping away at my Momma.
Her stucco laced with stress-filled days and trauma
Her street corners full of these kids, my friends, and their
    tragic signs
Who thought the only way to be alive was to be free from
    their minds.
So they sat there...
Dopin' up and gettin' high.
But my Momma always paid attention through and through
So she knew there were a few,
Who wanted so desperately to take in lives with a better
    view.
Who waited for the day when their stories didn't make
    her buildings shake
Or her windows break.

She wanted us to feel new and didn't want us to live just
    to survive.
She showed us places beyond poverty-stricken lives.
These people, these kids, my friends, who encountered a
    daily fight
Of nowhere to be, nowhere to go, nothing to eat.
And all along, the future we craved was beneath our own
    feet.
Momma showed us each crack on the sidewalk and told us,
"Pay attention to these streets...
Life ain't no crystal stair"
So appreciate each broken piece
Because the moment you see how each crack on the side-
    walk came to be,
You'll realize every crack began as something bigger than
    you and me.
So we walked carefully and kept eyes beneath our feet.
    People believing we
Had something to hide
But *really* we looked at each simple crack with beauty on
    our minds
And through all those
Bad blocks,
Bad days,
And mass graves
Beauty was a color we'd never seen before
It became our own hue
My town, my Momma
She wanted us to feel new
And some of us...
We pulled through.

Get Writing

Look in.

1. Emily's uncle said she was born with "no winning cards." Is there a defining statement someone in your family (or another) told you?
2. Whose love has made you strong?
3. How do you feel about the place where you grew up? Or where you live now?
4. How have you turned your losing cards into winning ones? How can you?

SHOUT out.

1. Write a letter to the city where you live or whichever one has influenced you the most.
2. Use rhyme to turn that letter into a poem.
3. Write a list of all the small things in your life that give you reason to smile.
4. Write an escape plan if you know you've got to get out of a place or a relationship so you can survive and thrive.

Claim your classic.

Classic Poems about Joy, Surviving, and Creating Your Own Worlds

"Eagle Poem," Joy Harjo
"Enough," Andrea Gibson

"Caged Bird," Maya Angelou

"Evolutionary Hymn," C. S. Lewis

"Haiku #4," Jill Scott

"I Think I'll Call It Morning," Gil Scott-Heron

"Phoenix," D. H. Lawrence

"Survival," Iris Tennent

"The Darkling Thrush," Thomas Hardy

"Where the Sidewalk Ends," Shel Silverstein

17

POSER

MAX TOUBES, 17

Max's Story

More often than not, the interests and passions I pursue are the few things that are actually *harder* for someone who has spent their entire life enjoying the spoils of white privilege. When I make hip-hop music and I color the lyrics with liberal undertones or opinions that people may consider "white abolitionist," the artists around me look at me like I'm trying to *be* black. The same thing happens when my songs are filled with profanities or if I use my voice in ways that sound different from how I talk. In reality, I'm not trying to *be* anything; I'm simply attracted to culture. And I'm disillusioned with whatever white-driven movement people think I should be part of instead.

My parents each grew up about an hour's drive from the dilapidated Bronx, where hip-hop was undergoing its genesis in the 1970s and '80s.

Grandmaster Flash and Afrika Bambaataa were spinning and scratching some of the first breaks while my dad practiced guitar to the north, in White Plains, New York. It's amazing that my parents could be so close to that movement and not be aware of its newfound cultural significance.

Regardless of their indifference to hip-hop, both of my parents were avid music fans. When I was little, they used to bump the Beatles and CSNY in the car more than anything. I was so obsessed with my parents' music, always eager to listen and expand my knowledge. I played the drums when I was small and began the guitar in the fifth grade (it's still a passion of mine). Around the age of three or four, I wouldn't even go by Max Toubes—I was John Winston Lennon—and I could regurgitate all kinds of historical dope about my childhood hero. I was a musicologist even in preschool.

I fell in love with hip-hop music and culture in seventh grade. Once introduced to hip-hop, I was enthralled and started emceeing after own-ing just one album: *The Eminem Show*. Once I realized I'd met the love of my life, however, I took it upon myself to expand my knowledge as thor-oughly as possible as I developed a cadence and style (I think my second album was *2001* and my third *Ready to Die*, and it was quite an adventure from there). I studied hip-hop more than I actually studied for school. But no matter how many documentaries I watched or biographies I read, nothing could ever beat listening.

I often found myself conflicted when artists I loved, like the Wu-Tang Clan and Lauryn Hill, openly expressed hatred toward white people like myself. Now I'm desensitized to it and content knowing that music is col-orless. I know I just have to put in more effort to prove myself. Now I'm used to walking out of places with the respect of strangers who hated me just for the color of my skin when I entered. A little backward for once—it feels nice.

By sophomore year, I was my school's resident rapper, and one morn-ing, I entered the auditorium, one earbud blaring Redman and a chip on my shoulder, to watch a "spoken word" assembly. I was faux skeptical—

acting like a rap god and telling my friends how there was no way these corny-ass Get Lit Players could have anything on my lyrical acrobatics! I'm the kind of person who doesn't like it when people come to my stomping grounds and try to one-up me at my own game (and at our school, my crew was the franchise, bangin' out tracks with our own beats and making little demos to pass around school). I sat down, puffed out my chest, and then . . . onto the stage walked Paul Mabon and Raul Herrera. Once Raul recited the first words of "Earthquake," I started paying attention. This was something I'd never seen teenagers do before, especially as profoundly and articulately as they were doing it. I was amazed. And though I was humbled by their performance, I was anything but discouraged. I started writing the kind of poetry I'd heard the Get Lit Players doing.

When I finally auditioned, I was nervous. I'd seen the Get Lit viral videos; I'd heard of their greatness at Brave New Voices. When I arrived at the office, I recognized the other new poets from an earlier competition. They were only the best of the best—the cream of the crop. I didn't know how I could compete. When I finally had my moment in front of the Get Lit administration (which included Raul and Paul from that first Blitz show), the head coach Matthew "Cuban" Hernandez told me to really try to show him who I was.

I thought to myself, *Damn! I've been practicing my poems all summer, but if this guy really wants to hear who I am* . . . Instead of reading what I'd planned, I busted out this verse I'd written that I thought was my best. It was all about the history of hip-hop, all in meter and rhyme. When I finished, a few people in the room gave me that same old look—like I was trying to be black. It made me nervous as I walked back down to the street. I took pride, however, in one aspect of the audition—even if some of them judged me, I left that office with the respect of everyone inside for my practiced lyrical ability.

When I eventually got the call from Cuban, I was jumping up and down in my head. I was so relieved to know that next year I'd be the kid at the Classic Slam that everybody knew.

Since my induction, the Get Lit Players have become a family to me. I love each and every one of my teammates like brothers and sisters, and I'm thrilled I've been able to work under the greatest modern poets to develop my skills.

Moreover, I'm fortunate that I found my love for poetry. I've been emceeing for years but only writing in other styles for about a year now. I write poetry as often as I can. Poetry saves my life on a daily basis, because even if you don't write a masterpiece every time, putting your emotions to words is one of the best ways to satisfy them. I'm proud of myself—when faced with adversity in my fields of interest, I was able to persevere and make my own name.

A few years ago, my dad took me to New York City. We went to 139th and Lenox Avenue in Harlem, where Big L was murdered. To 5Pointz Aerosol Art Center, just months before it was closed and painted over. And then we walked down to the Queensbridge Projects.

I'd asked him to take me to these places as a pilgrimage for the culture I'd adopted. (I'm lucky to have such an encouraging family.) The images I'd had in my mind of these places were alive with the colors of hip-hop street art and the movements of b-boys. But in reality, I saw that these areas were just run-down and decrepit. And I finally understood hip-hop better than I ever had before. I saw oppression and felt the need for a unifying hip-hop culture surge through me. I realized that hip-hop could never truly be mine. But I was content with the fact that a part of me, instead, belonged to hip-hop.

I am an artist. I am a guitarist, a producer, and a Get Lit Player. I am a creator, a writer, and a poet. I am Max, and only Max.

Classic Poem

Shout Out

Sekou Sundiata

Here's to the best words
In the right place
At the perfect time to the human mind
Blown-up and refined.
To long conversations and the
Philosophical ramifications of a beautiful day.
To the twelve-steppers
At the thirteenth step
May they never forget
The first step.
To the increase, to the decrease
To the do, to the do
To the did to the did
To the do to the did
To the done done
To the lonely.
To the brokenhearted.
To the new, blue haiku.
Here's to all or nothing at all.
Here's to the sick, and the shut-in.
Here's to the was you been to the is you in
To what's deep and deep to what's down and down
To the lost, and the blind, and the almost found.
To the crazy
The lazy
The bored
The ignored
The beginners

The sinners
The losers
The winners.
To the smooth
And the cool
And even to the fools.
Here's to your ex-best-friend.
To the rule-benders and the repeat offenders.
To the lovers and the troublers
The engaging
The enraging
To the healers and the feelers
And the fixers and the tricksters
To a star falling from a dream.
To a dream, when you know what it means.
To the bottom
To the root
To the base, uh, boom!
To the drum
Here's to the was you been to the is you in
To what's deep and deep to what's down and down
To the lost, and the blind, and the almost found.
Here's to somebody within the sound of your voice this morning.
*Here's to somebody who can't be within the sound of your voice
     tonight.*
*To a low-cholesterol pig sandwich smothered in swine without the
     pork.*
To a light buzz in your head
And a soundtrack in your mind
Going on and on and on and on and on like a good time.
Here's to promises that break by themselves

Here's to the breaks with great promise.

To people who don't wait in the car when you tell them to wait in
    the car.

Here's to what you forgot and who you forgot.

Here's to the unforgettable.

Here's to the was you been to the is you in

To what's deep and deep to what's down and down

To the lost, and the blind, and the almost found.

Here's to the hip-hoppers

The don't stoppers

Heads nodding in the digital glow

Of their beloved studios.

To the incredible indelible impressions made by the gaze as you gaze
    in the faces of strangers.

To yourself you ask: Could this be God? Straight up!

Or is it a mask? Here's to the tribe of the hyper-cyber

Trippin' at the virtual-most outpost at the edge on the tip

Believin' that what they hear is the mothership

Drawing near.

Here's to the was you been, to the is you in

To what's deep and deep, to what's down and down

To the lost, and the blind, and the almost found.

Response Poem

Hip-Hop Poem
Max Toubes

So maybe God created the heavens and the Earth
And then Adam and Eve showed him how humanity was
    never gonna work

And then Abram fathered Isaac, fathered Jacob, fathered Joseph

And led by Moses the Hebrews at long last reached their fucking holy land

Caesar was brought down by his own pious

After conquering Alexander of Macedon, who conquered Cyrus

And then Jesus was born in Judea to his mother, Mary

The Roman empire found his prospects rather scary

Then the Romans murdered Jesus and some of his apostles

But it wasn't long before Constantine was carrying the crosses

And the church was instated under Roman Catholicism

And all who didn't follow this system were accosted

Schism led to excommunication, misinterpretation, reformation

Movement led to more religious barriers between the nations

Generations passed and Columbus discovered the New World

And on a rare occasion ate with the Natives and didn't shoot first

The British were quick to colonize and antagonized folks again

Then captured West Africans and made them slaves to the white men

The Americans rebelled for freedom and succeeded

But after freedom fighting, the slave laws had still not
    been receded
Harriet Tubman led her people to safety
Lincoln emancipated them, but conditions diminished
    gravely

The media, then, murdered Gandhi and Malcolm for truth
    speaking
And after all of his progress it, too, reached Dr. Martin
    Luther King

John Lennon inspired a generation to imagine
Bob Marley taught the same kids to stand up for redemption
Marvin Gaye would ask what's going on with you
George Clinton united the nation under a groove
James Brown is considered the first emcee
But Hip-Hop began in 1973

When Kool Herc spun his break beats
And hip-hop traveled to parties and its popularity grew
    greatly
See hip-hop was not what Herc was intending to make
But hip-hop was not birthed as a mistake
Because hip-hop was not simply the music raw
Hip-hop was the writing on the walls
Hip-hop was the stand and the fall, the struggle and cause
Hip-hop was the b-boys and their cards, the emcees and
    their bars

And then the Sugarhill Gang bit everyone's rhymes
And shot hip-hop into the mainstream in 1979

When "Rapper's Delight" was getting played on popular music
    stations
And while many questioned this fad's presumed duration
It became Afrocentric and progressive back in NYC
And began to spread to other parts of the country
Pimps in ATL and gangstas in LA
And choppas in the Midwest began to earn their place
From '85 to like '97 that's what I think of as the Golden Age
Flourished like the renaissance there were so many names

Then geography and the media murdered Biggie and Pac
And it wouldn't be the first time a rapper beefed and got
    popped
And it wouldn't be the last time the pigs let 'em get killed
    off
And some hip-hop lyrics just wasn't reason enough

Get Writing

Look in.

1. What traits did you inherit from each of your parents?
2. Is there something you want to say or do that the world doesn't expect or accept from you because of your race, gender, or age?
3. What have you done that you feel most proud of? Why?
4. What or who saves your life?
5. What is something you could never understand?

SHOUT out.

1. Write a poem about a world you don't belong to but would like to.
2. Write a poem to the creative icon in your life. A writer. A singer. An activist.

Claim your classic.

Poems about Finding Your Own Identity within Society and Hip-Hop

"Amethyst Rocks," Saul Williams

"An American Poem," Ras Baraka

"I Will Always Love H.E.R.," Alex Dang

"I'm a Rapper," Sekou Andrews

"Intellectual MCs," Michael Eric Dyson

"Letter to My 16-Year-Old Self," George Watsky

"My Best Friend Hip-Hop," Riva & Sciryl

"Sick and Tired," Shihan

"America," Tony Hoagland

"When Hip-Hop Was Fun," INQ

LONER

ZACHARY PERLMUTER, 18

Zach's Story

At a young age, I dealt with the divorce of my parents, a family full of alcoholics, and an urge to express myself by any means necessary. I was a fairly good student up until the seventh grade. Then I started slacking and hanging out with a crowd that was known to stir trouble, and it seemed to all go downhill from that point on. I didn't graduate in the middle school ceremony with the other kids up onstage, and it tore to shreds whatever bit of confidence I possessed. I started doing drugs and selling a bit because I thought that I would never amount to anything in life. At that point, my mind was made up: I was going to be just another sad excuse for a young man.

Right before I went to high school, my mom decided that it was time for a change and that we should move. So one summer day, while I was in

Canada visiting my dad, I got a call from her telling me about it—about how she thought it would be beneficial to my future if we left the place that supposedly provoked my rebellious side. Little did she know that separating me from everything I knew and loved was the most harmful thing she could do to my psyche.

When I first arrived in that dreadful new town, I felt nothing but hate and anger; I couldn't understand why she would do that to me. But I soon became a little less agitated because I met some kids that made my time spent there somewhat better.

Still, I hid behind a fake smile and lies that stretched for miles. I was absolutely positive that no one would ever want to associate with me if they knew how I really was. I would try my hardest to make people *not* want to be around me, and things went on this way for years, until my mom's boyfriend got so violent, she was forced to move us back to our hometown. That's when I met my teacher, Ms. Brenda Young, and my life changed forever.

Ms. Young is one of the biggest inspirations I have ever had the pleasure of meeting. She saw a side of me that I didn't even know existed. I used to write just to complete assignments, but then one day she told me that she thought the outcome could be something magical if I put my heart into what I was writing. After she told me that, I began to write poetry religiously. Every day and every night, I would either be on my phone writing or sitting in my dimly lit room with a notebook and a pencil. Then Ms. Young told me about a poetry competition called the Classic Slam that was organized by a wonderful program known as Get Lit—Words Ignite. As soon as I heard about that opportunity, I jumped in without a second thought.

While my school was preparing to compete in the Classic Slam, I dedicated every day toward perfecting my craft. I stayed after school to work on performance techniques and verbal exercises, and it was one of the most enjoyable times of my life. I didn't have any more time to break the law, to write on walls, to stay awake until I saw the sunrise; I was too busy falling in love with poetry and everything having to do with it. While we were training for the Slam, our team dealt with a lot of personal problems that seemed endless, but we always stayed together as a family. We never turned against each other no matter how hard it got. After rigorous training, I competed in the Slam with a classic poem titled, "What Horror to Awake at Night" by Lorine Niedecker because the words spoke to me and explained exactly how I was feeling. The message Lorine is trying to send with this poem is that even though she has some mundane routines and her time is usually occupied, it all means nothing. I responded with a poem titled "Nothing to Me," which describes my own personal definition of nothing. I did very well at the Classic Slam, and that day sealed my fate.

From then on, I was going to do whatever it took to make sure I was a professional poet.

Now I'm working with Get Lit as a Get Lit Player, which means that I visit many different schools around Southern California (and beyond) to promote literacy and positive attitudes. They are also training me as a Get Lit Mentor for the upcoming youth. As a matter of fact, I just helped my former teacher Ms. Young to coach my old school's Classic Slam team, and they made it all the way to the Grand Slam Finals (top four of forty teams), beating out thousands of other competitors. I thank Get Lit for helping me become the person I am today and for helping me figure out what I want to do in life, which is teach. (Thank you again, Get Lit, for helping me get my life back on track.)

Classic Poem

What Horror to Awake at Night
Lorine Niedecker
What horror to awake at night
and in the dimness see the light.
>*Time is white*
>*mosquitoes bite*
I've spent my life on nothing.

The thought that stings. How are you, Nothing,
sitting around with Something's wife.
>*Buzz and burn*
>*is all I learn*
I've spent my life on nothing.

I'm pillowed and padded, pale and puffing
lifting household stuffing—
>*carpets, dishes*
>*benches, fishes*
I've spent my life in nothing.

Response Poem

Nothing to Me
Zachary Perlmuter

To others, "nothing" is failure.
"Nothing" is the pure essence of laziness,
The result of never trying your hardest.
This angers the shit out of me!

What of the kid that was put in a horrible place,
Torn between parents with no positivity to embrace,
Raised by negativity, death, and neglect,
Mom's getting hair extensions with the welfare check,
Where's he learning respect,
And why is love seldom seen?
Marijuana, women, and graffiti fill this teen's dreams,
He says he feels nothing but an urge to cause mischief,
Covers up his pain with 40-ounces and paint missions.
The only people he trusts are the ones in his crew,
He doesn't believe in God because of what he's been
    through,
Women to him are nothing but a bunch of snakes,
Why be real in a world full of fakes?
His hand shakes when he's catching his tags,
Walking around South Central with paint-covered hands...
Barbed wire is like a goal he must complete,
Graffiti is a sport and he was borrrnnn to compete!
His mom asks,
"Why do you do this shit? It means nothing,
You'll just be another worthless vandal on the wall
That gets covered up and never seen again.
Do you do it for fame?
It makes you no money,
What's going on in your fucked up brain, *honey*?"

He leaves the room with tears behind his eyes,
Trying to force them out of their sockets, but he holds
    them back.
He leaves at three in the morning, dreaming of painting on
    train tracks with flat blacks

And shades of green, coming up with styles that no man's
    ever seen,
His pops says,
"Instead of doing a throw up, why don't you grow up?
I got you two job interviews and you didn't even show up.
You make me look bad in more ways than one...
The truth is I'm ashamed to call you my son."

So now the overwhelming feelings of loneliness and shame
    take over,
His brain pushing through the cocaine filters blocking nat-
    ural endorphins,
Preventing him from experiencing the slightest shred of
    happiness.
So that night he climbs the billboard,
Writes his final words,
And jumps.
For the seven seconds he was falling,
He had finally felt at peace.

"Another deceased vandal" is what the media said...
The news headline:
"Aren't you glad another worthless criminal is dead?"
His mom, crying hysterically at the funeral, grabs her son's
    lifeless body and screams,
"Please, oh God, please, say something to me, say something
    to me!"
And these final words were his response,

"What's something to you
Is nothing to me."

Get Writing

Look in.

1. Have you ever felt like you've "spent your life on nothing"?
2. What did you dream once that you'd be?
3. Do you feel rage toward anyone? A member of your family?
4. How have you been wronged? Does the person who's wronged you also wrong themselves?
5. Who or what has come to your rescue?

SHOUT out.

1. Write a poem, "I've Spent My Life On Something," and list all the things you've done (even/especially small things) that matter.
2. Write your epitaph (a short text that honors a deceased person) as if you are a third party writing about yourself. Write about your largest self—the person you hope or plan or wish to be.

Claim your classic.

Classic Poems About Rage, Death, and Loss of Innocence

"Acquainted with the Night," Robert Frost
"[Buffalo Bill 's]," E. E. Cummings
"George Gray," Edgar Lee Masters
"Grief Calls Us to the Things of This World," Sherman Alexie
"Nothing Gold Can Stay," Robert Frost

"On the Eve of His Execution," Chidiock Tichborne
"Piano," D. H. Lawrence
"The Geranium," Theodore Roethke
"Letters Found Near a Suicide," Frank Horne
"Vitae Summa Brevis Spem Nos Vetat Inchohare Longam,"
   Ernest Dowson

SCARRED

JAMIAH LINCOLN, 16

Jamiah's Story

I will never be normal.

When I was nine years old, I started developing keloids. (I'm sure the term is as unfamiliar to you as it was to me in the beginning.) No doctor could give me a straight answer. Now I know a keloid is a slightly raised patch of skin caused by an injury where the body produces too much tissue for protection. The scariest thing about my situation was that I was never injured. Maybe emotionally but never physically. These scars began to form all over my body—my back, arms, stomach, chest, abdomen—until they covered 40 percent of my skin. I was worried that maybe it was a serious medical problem. I felt overwhelmed and needed someone by my side.

Although there was no clear diagnosis, I began to see doctors to treat it. As my disease progressed, there was an urgency to treat what was occurring. I saw more than fifteen different doctors to get answers about this terrible affliction, but to this day, I've gotten nothing. There is no answer for why this is happening to me.

During middle school, kids constantly made fun of me and asked why my skin was the way it was. The questions made me question myself. I began to cover all of my rashes at any cost. Through steaming weather, I wore long sleeves.

I began looking for love and acceptance. I quit behaving because I didn't have to, and I was practically raising myself through all of this. My grades dropped dramatically, and I found myself hanging with the wrong people, going to the wrong places, and saying the wrong things.

At night, I'd sit alone and ask whatever superior being created us, "Why did this have to happen to me?" I didn't understand. There are seven billion people on the earth, and I was the one who was chosen to have this disease? No one could understand what I was going through, what I was feeling, because it wasn't occurring to them, only to me. It was hard for me to grasp how I was feeling. So I started writing about it. I wrote about my tears and disconnections. I wrote about the time I almost passed out when I covered up my scars in hundred degree weather. I wrote because I felt like writing took the scars away.

Just before eleventh grade, I began to show my arms and wear shorts during the summer. I noticed that people still asked me questions, but they didn't really judge me. It was only me who was judging myself. I still get asked a lot of questions, and occasionally, I get bullied and called "burnt" or "blackie." And sometimes I still question my beauty. But these days, I tend to stay positive about myself—or at least I try.

After finding what was most powerful in me—the most beautiful thing I have, regardless of my disease—I began to share it with the world: *my thoughts*. I searched all over to find an outlet for my poetry and I was blessed to discover Get Lit. The day I got onstage to share a poem about the public authorities abusing those of color, I forgot my lines. It was the first time I had ever been on a stage in front of people. I was nervous, shaking, and my heart beat louder than the gunshots killing my kind. I had to start the poem over again, and this time, I got through it. When I finished, I received the most life-changing applause I can remember.

I tried out to be a Get Lit Player. When I got the news that I had made the team, my bottled-up emotions broke the bottle. I was ready to conquer myself and change the world.

I will never be normal.

No one will ever understand the pain I endure when I wake up from a surgery and realize my condition will never go away. Abnormal runs in my blood. Procedure after procedure, it will never change. I will never be able to wear a bikini without someone staring at me, commenting on my flaws. I will never be able to go out without being questioned about the dark, raised patches on my skin. I will never be able to work out like my peers because my skin bleeds when I sweat. Overweight, attacked by my own body, and wishing to be normal—I will never understand why God chose me.

But I want to be heard. I want people to understand that constant struggle can destroy a soul quicker than the tide erodes the shore, quicker than a bullet stops the heart. I want those who struggle to understand that they can find themselves in their hardships. My struggle turned me upside down, punched me in the stomach, shot me in the foot. But once I fought and overcame my obstacle (which was self-pity over my situation), it went away. Maybe not forever, but when it comes back now, I know I can make it walk away again.

Overcoming this battle is what makes me a star. It has shown me the value in my soul. While it can be hard for me to recognize the good inside the disaster that is my body, now I know that originality is the key. And even when I don't know it, I *am* changing the world.

Normal is boring.

Classic Poem

I Am!
John Clare
I am—yet what I am none cares or knows;
My friends forsake me like a memory lost:
I am the self-consumer of my woes—
They rise and vanish in oblivious host,
Like shadows in love's frenzied stifled throes
And yet I am, and live—like vapours tossed

Into the nothingness of scorn and noise,
Into the living sea of waking dreams,
Where there is neither sense of life or joys,
But the vast shipwreck of my life's esteems;
Even the dearest that I loved the best
Are strange—nay, rather, stranger than the rest.

I long for scenes where man hath never trod
A place where woman never smiled or wept
There to abide with my Creator, God,
And sleep as I in childhood sweetly slept,
Untroubling and untroubled where I lie
The grass below—above the vaulted sky.

Response Poem

Standing Tall
Jamiah Lincoln

It sucks to grow up
Infested by carelessness;

You're obligated to be surrounded by failure and such
You don't know if it's true when he says he loves you
You don't know if it's true when you hear she's with that
    dude.

So how do you cope?
How do you inhale negativity and exhale hope?
How do you smile through life when your feelings get shot
    before they roll off your tongue?

Ever since I've been here, things have changed,
My mind-set, motivation, tolerance for pain.

What am I doing?
Making my brain insane instead of making it great,
Turning into the animals that sit along this crate.
I hold my arms up, legs out, and open my mouth,
And tell society to eat my soul.

I give away the beauty inside me until I grow old,
Or until I die young.
I think,
Is this how I sprung?
How I bloomed?
Set for failure too?
I don't think so.

I'd rather make something positive of myself.
I'd rather be this ball of good vibes for the ones in need to
    feed off of,
I'd rather be the girl who cuts up her heart and gives it to
    people who have lost pieces of theirs,

I want to fix those previous-night cry affairs,
I want to share my passion,
I want to fix the girl that cuts on accident,
I want to love the one that holds my hand no matter what.
She's the one that keeps me sane...
I want to hug the one that throws reality at my face and
      tells me things will be okay.
She keeps away the pain...

I want to thank the one that provides me with happiness,
      bliss, and the truth,
He gives me hope.

I want to pray for the ones who stabbed me all over with
      their pessimistic views,
Who grabbed me by my feet,
And took me to hell for just a split second,
The ones so low they've given up on standing tall,
I pray one day,
You'll get up.

Get Writing

Look in.

1. Is there some condition you have that you hide or try to hide from others?
2. What are your wounds that people see, and what are your wounds that are below the surface?

3. What about your life makes you ask *Why me?* most often?

4. What is normal?

5. What battle have you overcome that makes you a star?

SHOUT out.

1. Write a poem about how you turn against yourself or are your own worst enemy.

2. Write a poem about how you accept yourself exactly as you are.

Claim your classic.

Classic Poems about the Pain of Life and the Act of Overcoming

"Fatality," Ruben Dario

"If," Rudyard Kipling

"*Invictus*," William Ernest Henley

"Life Doesn't Frighten Me," Maya Angelou

"Life Is Fine," Langston Hughes

"Our Hearts Should Do This More," Hafiz

"Saint Francis and the Sow," Galway Kinnell

"Still I Rise," Maya Angelou

"The Uses of Sorrow," Mary Oliver

"There Is Another Sky," Emily Dickinson

The wound is where the light enters us.

—Rumi

WANNABE

DiANE LUBY LANE

Diane's Story

I believe we all have a responsibility to change the world, or to leave it better than we found it . . . at least our little portion, our little spot. I live in Los Angeles. I am an okay actress with stage fright. I am an okay writer with boxes of journals stored in the attic. I am a teacher without a college degree. I am the founder and executive director of a teen literary non-profit without any prior experience in business management. I am a lover of human beings, and this is where I shine. I have a calling. Is it to save teen literacy in Los Angeles? Well . . . it is to love the people I see beside me. Specifically teenagers. And let them know that they are smart. And capable. And worth something. And required to better the world.

Recently I attended a Women in the World Summit (WITW) at Lincoln Center in New York, where one of our Get Lit Players—

185

Marquesha (who you met in the pages of this book)—was performing. WITW was created by Tina Brown in association with the *New York Times*. It is a three-day convening of female leaders and supporters who gather to discuss women's rights, empowerment, and issues. The elite of the elite show up for this thing—I'm talking Meryl Streep, Angelina Jolie, Alicia Keys, Ken Burns, Malala Yousafzai, as well as ordinary movers and shakers from all over the world. Each featured speaker is interviewed by an equally powerful and awe-inspiring moderator. The stories blew my mind! "Untouchables" from India rejecting that label and claiming the word "Dalits"; Pussy Riot from Russia taking on Putin and demanding rights for all; Jimmy Carter championing women's issues and starting what he called "the most important work of his life" at ninety!

I was in the second row and what struck me about the moderators (almost as much as their razor-sharp intelligence) was their rock-hard, shiny calves that caught the light and *gleamed* from up onstage. Were these women reporters or triathletes? Did rock-hard, shiny, *naked* calves come with their Ivy League degrees? Whatever happened to panty hose? And what did this say of my own razor-stubbled cankles hidden (I thought smartly) beneath a pair of thick stockings and boots? IT WAS THIRTY-TWO DEGREES OUTSIDE! DID I MISS THE MEMO? WERE ROCK-HARD CALVES A PREREQUISITE TO SUCCESS???

Missing the discussion of rape in the military, my mind turned to ponder my own inferior calves. It made perfect sense. These world-shaking overachievers were the ones up bright and early during their Columbia days, rowing or running, rain or shine. They were strong. They were hearty. They played competitive sports—blond ponytails wagging, adoring fathers encouraging them from up in the stands. Jetting from shore houses to ski trips, creating that all-too-precious commodity: confidence.

The things you know us by, are simply childish.
Beneath it is all dark, it is all spreading, it is unfathomable deep;

> but now and again we rise to the surface
> and that is what you see us by.
> —*To the Lighthouse*, Virginia Woolf

Thank you Virginia for shedding light on the plight of the poor misunderstood triathlete/reporters up on stage!

But what if she's right? Sometimes we make too much of people's bright spots—their intelligence, cleverness, accomplishments (calves!). Maybe their real power comes from a different source entirely.

I use poetry to help young people feel better about themselves. And maybe I'm moved to help them because my teen years were where it all went "wrong" for me—or "right," depending upon how you look at it. That was the time when my father remarried, and I lost him. I didn't lose him exactly, but our relationship shifted, and I saw him a small fraction of the time I was used to. This was the single most traumatic experience of my life.

My father was smart (class valedictorian), handsome (think Clark Kent/Superman), engaging (think a young Bill Clinton), and my hero. Before my father remarried, my brother Rich and I (Rich is eleven months younger than me, so that makes him my "Irish twin") spent one weekend a month with him and a few weeks over the summer. Driving from New Jersey (my home) to his in Hartford, Connecticut, we'd stopped in New York for Yankees games, Chinese New Year parades, and to visit our relatives in New Rochelle. This time with my dad was my second life—my exotic one—with my favorite person in the world. Rich and I would fight for who got to sit next to him on the powder-blue velour seat of his Oldsmobile (and when I'd win, I'd curl up and fall asleep with my head on his leg). Having a father—for a daughter or for a son—is one of the most important experiences a child can have. I know because the lack of having one is the single most written-about topic by teenagers.

My father loved to read, like I do. He thought I was smart. He listened to my nonstop talking and called me a "chatterbox." He was my advocate in this world—the one who thought I was special. (Everybody needs someone who thinks they're special.) And when he got remarried, that was gone. He told himself that we were teenagers who no longer needed him, but that couldn't have been further from the truth. There was my mother in the stands to watch my brother Rich pitch his World Series games, my brother to walk me down the aisle in a "Miss Teenage America" pageant (yes, it was as awful as it sounds), and boys to fill the empty spot created by his absence.

A first shot of pain. A first hole. Here it is. This loss was my first real teacher. I cried every day for over a year, and in the eighth grade, it took the form of formal depression—only I didn't know what it was. I couldn't think straight. My grades went from As and Bs to Cs and Ds. I just wanted to sleep. Kids in school started making fun of me, refusing to sit next to me or be on my team in gym, calling me "airhead." I ate lunch in a bathroom stall and hid in gym lockers until after teams were picked. I called it the fog; I couldn't see my way out of it. All I could do was pray—which I did, every single day for over a year—that it would lift.

And then it did. But it took a long, long time, and by that time, the damage was done. I was scarred. "Beauty" was a lifeline delivered unexpectedly, out of nowhere. It's amazing what losing your braces and gaining some weight can do. People became nicer. Boys were finally interested in me. I felt some power and less invisible. I loved a boy who wore parachute pants and a leather jacket. He liked to drink and his nickname was "Puke," but he taught me the lyrics to every Run DMC song and tutored me on the math portion of my SATs. I dated him for three years. Walking up and down the boardwalk at the Jersey Shore, he'd say in his thick New Jersey accent, "Isn't my girl HOT?" Charming, I know. But his tenderness saved me. And I had a strong mother who was one of the top salespeople in the country at a Fortune 500 company. Her success gave me a sense of identity and legacy—"You're Barbara Luby's daughter! Wow!" But it couldn't sate that void.

There are some wounds that will never heal. You live with them. They throb. A feeling of something "not there" that oddly enough becomes, in its way, more real than the things that are there. And this lack has as much to do with who we become as our accomplishments. If only we can stay afloat. If only they don't take us under.

And this is why I love teenagers. Perhaps I am returning to the scene of my own damage and demise though ultimate purpose: to find that little girl on the side of the road and tell her, "Don't fall. You didn't get the whole message. You are actually perfect!"

I heard Dr. Cornel West say to a recognized group of leaders, "We are all here because somebody loved us." So at Get Lit, once a child is steadied and seen, they must go out into the world to steady and see others. That's the deal. The goal. The work. To share this truth and to Love. Not with a small and dinky "l" but with a capital "L."

We (at Get Lit) are warriors of love. Of action. Of remembering, or putting back together the pieces of who we are. Remembering our wholeness before we accepted the lie that we were less than perfect. And we use poetry (and excerpts of literature) to do it.

I imagine the people who take action AND have shiny calves, paid-off debts, and college degrees, and some days I am ashamed I am not them. Some days, I want to stop all I am doing because HOW DARE I DO WHAT I'M DOING WHILE NOT HAVING THESE THINGS! I MUST HAVE THEM TO ACT! I MUST!

And maybe someday I will.

But for today, I stuff my cankles into a pair of stocking-lined boots and trudge out there to have a go—a real go—at existence!

Classic Poem

From Jazz by Toni Morrison
He needs courage for that, but he has it. He has the courage to do what duchess of Marlborough do all the time: relinquish being an adored bud clasping its future, and dare to open wide, to let the layers of its petals go flat, show the cluster of stamens dead center for all to see.

Response Poem

Where Do You Hear the Voice?
Diane Luby Lane

Where do you hear the Voice?
So Beautiful it pulls you Out of yourself and Into everything
　　else
So you can't tell where you end and somebody else begins
You ain't this and you ain't that
You're All of it
Where do you go to feel Good?
Where are you Grand? Where are you Glorious?
What Place gives you Joy, Soul, Spirit, Juice, Goods, Now, Zip,
　　Zap, Fizz,
Fly, Kiss, Pop, Woe, Wow, Life, Liven, Love, Pizzaz,
Yeah, All right, Ah-ha, Hallelujah!
Where can you Spread-out, Lay-down, Lay-low, Open-up,
　　Drip-drop, Expand, Extract—
Meaning, Goodness, Beauty, Worlds, Whys, How-comes,
　　Why-nots?
Where is your Joy?

What makes you Happy?

Fill yourself Up in that place that fills you 'cause you've
done left paradise

Now you're in the garden with the traps and the rats and
the cats

But don't be afraid!

Spread your arms out—

Take a Risk!

Let the Petals of your flower go flat for the
Whole Wide World to see!

Lay it Down! Give it Up! Get it Out!

You came here with love, so Love!

Open up your Arms to the lepers, and the outcasts, and the
tax collectors —

Open up!

That's right!

It's okay to feel lonely and forgotten, small, angry,
meaningless, confused, forsaken—

Reach your fingers out!

So far—

Further!

Past the pain—

Till you've pulled yourself apart and all that's left of you is

One Heart Beating with the Universe—

You hear it?

Oh yeah

Where you hear it?

Cousteau heard it in the Ocean

Goodall heard it with the Chimps

Marley in the Music

Where do you hear it?
Glorious, glorious Lovelies—
Remember

Who you are!

Get Writing

Look in.

1. Have you ever felt a great, overwhelming joy? Where do you think it comes from?
2. Do you feel a calling to do something specific?
3. Is there something that everyone else has that you're ashamed you don't?
4. Where do you think we come from?
5. How has a past hurt given your life purpose and direction?
6. Where do you hear the voice that connects you to something larger than yourself?

SHOUT out.

1. Write a poem about your purpose. Make it a personal mission statement.
2. Write about the part of yourself you most compare to others. Include how you finally come to peace with being different or even less than in certain areas.
3. Write about a wound that has given you power.

Claim your classic.

Poems About Living Awakened Lives

"Be Still," Arthur Osborne

"Dazzling and Tremendous . . ." from "Song of Myself," *Leaves of Grass*, Walt Whitman

"Fairy-Tale Logic," A. E. Stallings

"i thank You God for most this amazing," E. E. Cummings

"Life," Juan Ramón Jiménez

"So Much Happiness," Naomi Shihab Nye

"The Journey," Mary Oliver

"The Man Watching," Rainer Maria Rilke

"The Moment," Margaret Atwood

"With That Moon Language," Hafiz

ALIVE
JAMIAH LINCOLN AND MIRIAM SACHS

Jamiah and Miriam wrote "Alive" in response to the episode "Untitled" of HBO's *Six Feet Under*. They first performed the poem at Dodger Stadium for Get Lit's "The Poetry of Television" event where we honored Alan Ball with our IGNITE Award and responded poetically to some of the most iconic shows on television.

ALL: I am trying to sleep.
J: My eyes see shapes and his won't leave
My throat is closed it's hard to breathe

ALL: I feel like I am going to die.

J: He left me
He dug a hole through me like a bullet in slow motion.
ALL: I don't know what to do
M: You can do anything. You're alive...
ALL: What's a little pain compared to that?

ALL: In complete darkness you hear only one thing

M: A beat at a rhythm in which your body chooses to go
ALL: Your blood chooses to pump
M: Your heart chooses to rapidly remind you
ALL: You are alive.

M: It is impossible, no matter how hard we try, to explain this
ridiculous miracle. This body, these atoms that dance in
and out of each other,

ALL: In complete darkness.

J: That beat is the opportunity to smile
M: The opportunity to fall in love
J: The way that we fall.

ALL: Literally.

J: Without seeing the crack we slipped up on,
ALL: The missed step
Literally, sputtering, spitting onto the pavement.
You hear only one thing.

J: The opportunity to become
M: A doctor
J: A photographer
M: An astronaut

ALL: The opportunity to create a family

M: One mixed like cinnamon and nutmeg
J: Warm milk
ALL: And a hug or two when you come through the front
    door.
The opportunity to be successful...

J: In whatever you strive for,
whatever your heart beats for.
ALL: Although the world is a profoundly heartless place
In complete darkness you hear only one thing.

A beat.

And you can do anything...
You
Are
Alive.

HOW TO START YOUR OWN POETRY GROUP

Join the Revolution!

Thousands of students write poems with Get Lit every year, and the program is expanding to more schools, states, and countries faster than ever. It's never been easier to make an impact on your community at home or to share your art with the world. Here are some ways to get involved.

1. Be the change (start your own program)!

- Create a workshop: Gather a group of your friends, and use the "Get Writing" prompts in this book to get going. You could also start an extracurricular club or program using the Get Lit curriculum.

- Host an Open Mic: We dare you to host an Open Mic at a venue in your town. Many places (schools, restaurants, rec centers) will donate the space. Invite your friends and family members, create a sign-up sheet, and let people jump onstage and perform. You can even start the show with a preplanned performance or showcase, to ensure the quality is great.
- Gathering the masses: Don't forget to promote your programs and events with postcards, emails, and social-media campaigns. A revolution is only as great as its members!

2. Seek a mentor for help.

- Who in your life would be amazing at facilitating a poetry workshop? Maybe a stellar teacher at your school, a counselor at your camp? It should be someone who seems to give you permission to be your best self, that asks questions about your life, and that seems to earn respect. It could even be you! The curriculum is portable and can easily be set up in any institution across the globe.
- You can order a LIT KIT at getlit.org. The great thing about starting a spoken word community is that you don't need a lot of materials. You just need dedicated participants, a designated leader/mentor/teacher, and a plan. And, of course, a place to write!

3. We are always here for you.

When we say that your voice matters, we really mean it!

- If you're ever in Los Angeles, come check out our events! We hold a Poetic Convergence in the fall, a Classic Slam in the spring, and an Open Mic every month at the Actors' Gang!
- Check out our YouTube channel (www.youtube.com/GLword signite) to get inspiration for themes, choreography, and other

performance tips! You can also email us to find an after-school spoken word program near you.

- If you upload a poem to YouTube and email us the link at info@ getlit.org, we may choose to post it on a brand-new playlist called "The Literary Riot," where your poetry will be viewed by thousands of poets and fans.
- Send us a written poem. We will compile our favorites and include them as bonus works in our 2016–17 anthology, alongside the work of our own Get Lit Players.

Guidelines for Working with Classic Poems

1. Learn the process.

Claim Your Classic

Memorize & Perform Classic

Write & Memorize Individual Response

Write & Memorize Group Response

Rehearse & Perform!

2. Claim your poem.

This is what we call the process of finding a poem you're going to learn and recite. Some ways to know it when you hear it are:

- A word/phrase might JUMP out at you.
- It might make you FEEL something.
- You might feel or hear a YES inside you.
- It might make you want to LEARN more about it.

- You might like the RHYTHM.
- It might EXPRESS how you feel about something.
- You might picture yourself PERFORMING it.

3. Memorize.

Once each person in your group has their classic poem, begin to prepare it for performing.

- Learn about the author.
- Decide who you are reciting your poem to (deciding that you're reciting it to a relative or a certain friend could make your delivery more meaningful).
- Memorize it.

Why memorize? When you memorize something, it's with you forever. It flows in your blood and beats with your heart. It becomes a part of you.

4. Overmemorize!

Know your classic poem inside and out.

5. Perform.

Begin by reciting a poem yourself. It can be a short one. Demonstrate the order by saying your name, the name of the poem, the poet's name, a little bit about the poet, and reciting the poem.

Writing a Response Poem

Your poem awaits in the space between your pen and your journal. For example: Anne Sexton wrote "The Big Heart" in response to a line from an essay by Yeats, and Etheridge Knight wrote "The Sun Came" in response to Gwendolyn Brooks's poem "Truth."

Be aware of your audience and yourself when you read your response poems.

- Notice your own reaction and the reaction of the people in your group. Is the poem finished? Have you evoked strong feelings in others? Have you revealed yourself? Has your response answered some part of the original poem?
- Give notes to each other—all positive, all constructive. (What line/part stands out? What is your favorite part? Is everyone clear about what you are saying? Could it be more specific? What is unclear?)
- Rewrite your first draft by putting the strong lines on their own fresh sheet of paper and rework the weaker lines by making them more specific, checking for overall flow.
- If the poem feels finished, then memorize it.
- If it needs rewriting, keep working on it. Remember: the best writing is rewriting.

Group Work

Group poems can be so inspiring. The purpose of group poems is to learn to work together and to cocreate a work of art. It is also a chance to heighten the delivery of a poem by playing with the choral arrangement—using many voices rather than one. If possible, watch or listen to a professional group performance.

Each group should divide their poem with lines marked by character, like a dialogue in a play. (Note: the more intricately broken up the poem is, the more impressive it will be.)

If there's a book that you want to read but it hasn't been written
yet, then you must write it.

—Toni Morrison

Sharing Poems Publicly

Sharing poems with others is a powerful force. Whether you're in it for
the applause, the activism, or both, this process is not complete until
you've performed your poem live. Once you have a set of five to ten
poems, this is your "repertoire." You are ready to speak at local events
and even travel, sharing your words with the audiences that need and
want to hear them.

Sisters
Walter Finney and Kyland Turner

Walter and Kyland wrote "Sisters" in response to the fights that they have with their own sisters, their participation in a march against sex trafficking, and their work on a group performance of "Dark August" by Derek Walcott. If you look closely, you can see all of these things in this poem as a response.

All: HERE WE GO WITH THIS AGAIN

Walter: I'm awakened by the relentless shaking of her beads as she jumps up and down and pulls one of my socks off my feet. Kamaya, get out my room!

Kyland: Dammit, Simone, how many times do I have to tell you? No you cannot use my remote.

ALL: OUR SISTERS ARE ANNOYING AS HELL.

Walter: Even when all hell is breaking loose...Mama and Daddy arguing over bills, and here she comes with this...

Kyland (as Kamaya): Walter, can I have a dollar?

Walter: No!

Walter (as Simone): Kyland, do you think I would die if I drink this soap water?

Kyland: Simone, you have got to be kidding me, asking questions while the dishes are being thrown? This is not the time.

Walter: Close my door.

ALL: WE GET IT, THEY'RE LITTLE GIRLS.

Walter: But if I hear one more...

Kyland (as Kamaya): Walter can I use your phone to play Candy Crush

Walter: No!

Walter (as Simone): Kyland, if you don't want your burger, can I have it?

Kyland: Man, I'm starving.

ALL: THEY AGGRAVATE US DAILY. WE CAN SEE WHY OUR DADDIES LEFT.

Kyland: But sometimes it hurts knowing the only male figure in my sister's life is a 18-year-old with 12-year-old tendencies. Engaging in arguments...

(Walter makes farting sound)

Kyland: Simone, did you just fart?

Walter: I mean, I love Kamaya, I do, but I hate stepping on those Barbie dolls every time I take a shower. But I hope she knows she can be stripped and sold like the toys she's always leaving around, because in some parts of the world couples are only permitted to have one child.

ALL: BUT IN AMERICA, SOME CHILDREN ARE ONLY PERMITTED TO ONE PARENT.

Kyland: What if I was the only child? No one to ask for my remote to change from MTV.

Walter: What if I woke up to see my sister on the news missing? What if my sister was one of the 150,000,000 little girls and women lost to human trafficking?

Kyland: What if I scream bring back my sister? Would TV be so important then?

ALL: WE PROTECT THEM

Walter: Accept them, wish to neglect them but we can't, we must provide for them.

Kyland: Man, but I can't. I swear I'm not my father. I didn't marry my mother, I came from her. I can't work a 9–5, I'm in school from 8–3. Eight hours I can't provide.

ALL: BUT I'M SLOWLY LEARNING

Kyland: To love the black days

Walter: Like the sunny days of spring even though you bring thunderstorms to my parade sometimes

ALL: RAINING DOWN A MILLION QUESTIONS

Walter (as Simone): Kyland, can I see your remote?

Kyland (as Kamaya): Walter, can I have a dollar?

Walter (as Simone): Kyland, can you buy me something?

Kyland (as Kamaya): Walter, are you going to leave like my daddy did?

Walter (as Simone): Kyland, why are you always gone?

Kyland (as Kamaya): Walter, how old are you?

Walter (as Simone): Kyland, aren't you 18?

Kyland (as Kamaya): Walter, do you pay the bills?

Walter (as Simone): Kyland, can you cook?

ALL: ARE YOU MY REAL BROTHER? WHY DO WE HAVE DIFFER-ENT DADDIES? WHERE'S MY MAMA AT? DO YOU REALLY LOVE ME LIKE YOU SAY YOU DO? MY DADDY SAID THE SAME THING.

Kyland: He used to hold my sister in the center of his palm, but now I hold you in the center of this poem.

ALL: MY SISTER.

Walter: I'm gonna make it on my own. My daddy never taught me, just like yours, he was gone.

ALL: BUT I'M STILL HERE TO ANSWER YOUR QUESTIONS.

Kyland: Simone, take my remote.

Walter: Here, Kamaya, you can have a dollar.

Kyland: You can have the rest of my burger.

Walter: No, I'm not going nowhere.

Kyland: I'm always gone 'cause I'm too busy writing these poems.

Walter: I'm only 19.

Kyland: Yes, I'm 18.

Walter: I pay the bills, when I got the money.

Kyland: No, I can't cook.

ALL: YES, WE'VE ALWAYS BEEN HERE. NO, I'M NOT LEAVING LIKE HIM. I LOVE YOU. MY SISTER.

200 POEMS TO CRACK YOU OPEN

Elizabeth Alexander
> "Race"

Sherman Alexie
> "Grief Calls Us to the Things
> of This World"
> "On the Amtrak from Boston
> to New York City"

Sekou Andrews
> "I'm a Rapper"

Maya Angelou
> "Caged Bird"
> "Life Doesn't Frighten Me
> At All"
> "Phenomenal Woman"
> "Still I Rise"

Margaret Atwood
> "The Moment"
> "A Sad Child"
> "Variation on the Word
> Sleep"

"i thank You God for most
this amazing"
"maggie and milly and molly
and may"
"next to of course god
america i"

Alex Dang
"I Will Always Love H.E.R."

Ruben Dario
"Fatality"

Emily Dickinson
"I Had Been Hungry All the
Years"
"I'm Nobody! Who Are
You?"
"The Lost Jewel"
"Me! Come! My Dazzled
Face"
"There Is Another Sky"

Gregory Djanikian
"Mrs. Caldera's House of
Things"

John Donne
"No Man Is an Island"

Ernest Dowson
"*Vitae Summa Brevis Spem
Nos Vetat Incohare Longam*"

Michael Eric Dyson
"Intellectual MCs"

T. S. Eliot
"*La Figlia Che Piange*" (The
Weeping Girl)

Ralph Waldo Emerson
"Success"

Rhina Espaillat
"Bilingual/Bilingüe"
"Weighing In"

Robert Frost
"Acquainted with the Night"
"Nothing Gold Can Stay"

Kahlil Gibran
"On Reason and Passion"

Andrea Gibson
"Enough"
"Jewelry Store"

Jack Gilbert
"Failing and Flying"

Allen Ginsberg
"Howl"
"Song"
"A Supermarket in California"

Nikki Giovanni
"I Wrote a Good Omelet"

Edgar Albert Guest
"The Little Orphan"

Hafiz
"Dropping Keys"
"How Does It Feel to Be a
Heart?"
"Our Hearts Should Do This
More"
"With That Moon Language"
"Your Beautiful Parched,
Holy Mouth"

Thomas Hardy
"The Darkling Thrush"

Joy Harjo
"Eagle Poem"
"Remember"
"She Had Some Horses"

**Alysia Harris and Aysha
El Shamayleh**
"HIR"

Robert Hayden
"Those Winter Sundays"

William Ernest Henley
"Invictus"

Juan Felipe Herrera
"Song Out Here"

Tony Hoagland
"America"

Frank Horne
"To Mother"

Langston Hughes
"A Dream Deferred"
"Dream Variations"
"Ennui"
"Life Is Fine"

Zora Neale Hurston
"How It Feels to Be Colored
Me"

INQ
"When Hip-Hop Was Fun"

Juan Ramon Jimenez
"Life"

Ha Jin
"Ways of Talking"

Lenore Kandel
"Age of Consent"
"Small Prayer for Fallen
Angels"

Galway Kinnell
"Saint Francis and the Sow"

Rudyard Kipling
"If—"

Etheridge Knight
"Belly Song"

Kendrick Lamar
"Mortal Man"

D. H. Lawrence
"All I Ask"
"Phoenix"
"Piano"

C. S. Lewis
"Evolutionary Hymn"

Audre Lorde
"Coping"
"Hanging Fire"
"Now"

Antonio Machado
"Last Night I Was Sleeping"

Haki Madhubuti
"destiny"

Edgar Lee Masters
"George Gray"

Marty McConnell
"Instructions for a Body"

Jeffrey McDaniel
"Letter to the Woman Who
Stopped Writing Me Back"
"The Archipelago of Kisses"
"The Secret"

Claude McKay
"If We Must Die"

Edna St. Vincent Millay
"I shall forget you presently,
my dear (Sonnet XI)"

Janice Mirikitani
"For a Daughter Who
Leaves"

Cherrie Moraga
"They Was Girls Together"

ABOUT THE CLASSIC POETS

Francisco X. Alarcón: Alarcón was a Chicano and American poet and educator. He is one of the few Chicano poets to have gained recognition within the United States while writing mostly in Spanish. His poetry—written in English, Spanish, and Nahuatl—is often presented to the reader in a bilingual format, and his work is minimalist in style.

Maya Angelou: One of America's most famous poets, Angelou was also an author, dancer, actress, playwright, director, singer, and civil-rights activist. She was widely known for her memoir *I Know Why the Caged Bird Sings*, which was the first nonfiction bestseller by an African American woman. She received more than fifty honorary degrees, and in 1993, at President Clinton's inauguration, recited her poem "On the Pulse of Morning."

Elizabeth Bishop: Bishop was an American poet and short-story writer whose work earned her several esteemed titles: Poet Laureate of the United States from 1949 to 1950, the Pulitzer Prize-winner for Poetry in 1956, and the National Book Award-winner in 1970. Bishop dedicated her 1965 volume of poems, *Questions of Travel*, to her longtime partner, the esteemed Brazilian architect Lota de Macedo Soares.

Charles Bukowski: An American poet born in Germany, Bukowski's brusk, short style became the voice of his generation. His work addressed the ordinary lives of poor Americans, sexual encounters, and the drudgery of work. Bukowski was a cult hero, relying on experience, imagination, direct language, and violent and sexual imagery in his work, making him an iconic yet controversial figure today.

John Clare: Clare was an English poet known for his celebratory representations of the English countryside and his melancholia about modernization. He is now considered to be among the most important nineteenth-century poets. Clare was not a fan of punctuation, although many publishers felt the need to remedy this practice in the majority of his work.

Leonard Cohen: Cohen is an iconic Canadian poet and musician. His songs and poems are sensual, spiritual, and hymn-like. Cohen received a Grammy Award for lifetime achievement in 2010 and released his thirteenth studio album, *Popular Problems*, on September 22, 2014—a day after his eightieth birthday.

Sierra DeMulder: DeMulder is an internationally touring performance poet and educator, and founder of Button Poetry (the largest digital distributor of spoken word in the world). A two-time National Poetry Slam champion, she has published two collections of poetry. She also works as the curriculum director of the Gustavus Adolphus College Institute of Spoken Word and Poetry Slam, affectionately known as "Slam Camp."

Langston Hughes: A revolutionary American poet, playwright, and social activist and one of the pioneers of the Harlem Renaissance, Hughes was one of the earliest innovators of jazz poetry, and he inspired a generation of artists and writers to own and appreciate black culture. His ashes are interred beneath the entrance of the Arthur Schomburg Center for Research in Black Culture in Harlem, with an inscription of one of his lyrics: "My soul has grown deep like the rivers."

D. H. Lawrence: Lawrence was an English novelist, poet, playwright, essayist, and literary critic. His works explore the issues of emotional health, vitality, spontaneity, instinct, and the dehumanizing effects of modernity and industrialization. A bohemian at his core, he lived a life of wanderlust, which took him to many places including a long residence in New Mexico.

Henry Wadsworth Longfellow: One of the five Fireside Poets—the first American poets whose popularity rivaled that of British poets—Longfellow was best known for his lyric poetry, but he experimented with many forms. His work often has a musical quality and depicts mythological stories and legends.

Toni Morrison: A groundbreaking American novelist, editor, and professor, Morrison brought core narratives of the female African American experience to the forefront of American literary culture. Among her best known novels are *The Bluest Eye, Sula, Song of Solomon,* and *Beloved*. She won the Pulitzer Prize in 1988 for *Beloved* and the Nobel Prize in 1993. On May 29, 2012, she received the Presidential Medal of Freedom. Today, she serves as professor emeritus at Princeton University and continues to write.

Lorine Niedecker: Niedecker was a Wisconsin poet whose work is praised for its spare language and vivid imagery and has been compared to the work of Chinese and Japanese writers. She lived in the wilderness most of her life and wrote in seclusion. Her closest friends and relatives didn't even know she was a poet. Her work was overlooked until late in her life. Today she is considered an important voice in contemporary American poetry.

Marge Piercy: Piercy is an American novelist, poet, and social activist. Jewish symbols and imagery are at the heart of her work. Extremely prolific, Piercy has written more than seventeen novels and nineteen volumes of poetry. Her poetry often addresses feminist issues and is communicated through highly personal free verse. Her novels express a passion for social change and for *tikkun olam*, which is Hebrew for "repairing the world."

Tadeusz Różewicz: A Polish poet, dramatist, and writer, Różewicz was one of the great Eurpoean witness poets whose life was profoundly affected by the events of the twentieth century, including World War I and World War II. He is considered one of the most creative continuators of the Polish and international avant garde.

Sonia Sanchez: An African American poet and author most often associated with the Black Arts Movement, Sanchez is an activist for racial equality and the first to create and teach a course based on black women and literature in the United States. Sanchez is known for her unique combining of musical sounds (like scatting) with traditional poetic formats (like haiku and tanka).

Michele Serros: Serros was a Chicana author, poet, and comedic social commentator who wrote several books that have become required reading in Chicano studies programs. Her poetry and prose was influenced by both her working-class Mexican American heritage and Southern California pop culture. She is part of what has come to be known as Generation Mex.

Anne Sexton: Sexton was an American poet famous for the personal nature of her verse. Her work is usually grouped with other confessional poets like Robert Lowell and Sylvia Plath. In 1967, her book *Live or Die* won the Pulitzer Prize for poetry. She was known for her bouts of depression and severe mental illness. She eventually committed suicide.

Sekou Sundiata: An African American poet and performer known for works that combined poetry, music, and drama, Sundiata released several albums and was nominated for a Grammy Award. He was a Sundance Institute Screenwriting Fellow, as well as the first writer-in-residence at the New School University in New York. His one-man show, *Blessing the Boats*, was based upon his experiences of heroin addiction, a car crash, and a kidney transplant from a friend.

Walt Whitman: Often called the father of free verse, Whitman is one of America's most significant poets. Whitman's poetry celebrated both his body and his soul and found beauty even in death. Part of *Leaves of Grass* (a landmark in the history of American literature) called "Song of Myself" is written in an all-powerful first-person narration. He never took his hat off for anyone because he believed all humans were created equal.

STAND CLEAR
WALTER FiNNIE, BRIAN MARTINEZ, AND KYLAND TURNER

"Stand Clear" was born when Kyland and Walter were performing poems and freestyling on a train. The finished product won the Youth Speaks national Raise Up Project contest and was performed at the Kennedy Center and the White House.

ALL: Stand clear — the doors are closing

W: I ride this Blue Line every Saturday

Sort of a blue mind that won't go away

Last week I got jumped,

ALL: This week I'm not afraid

W: Instead I patiently wait to take the ride of my life

My weekly routine

ALL: But now my train has arrived

Stand clear — the doors are closing

B: Like options

The reason I ride this bus

ALL: Every morning is a must

B: I'm tired and I'm hungry

Wish that I could grab some lunch

I'm on a mission for a kitchen and my vision is rich

I gotta do it for my mother,

ALL: I'm no longer a kid

B: so for tonight I'm riding busses that smell like...

ALL: Stand clear — the doors are closing

K: I've been waiting for this bus for 30 minutes

ALL: Practice starts at 2, I fell asleep at 2,

K: it's a 2-hour bus ride

I'm hoping the driver will let me slide

ALL: like skates on ice

K: Maybe if I ask nice

Like, Driver, my ambition is your job title

And in my backpack under my bible is the law

ALL: so I know my rights

He doesn't want to hear no excuses

Stand clear — the doors are closing

W: This commute is my life

ALL: **Fast with brief stops**

W: In the belly of the beast

I'm just trying to make it out

Skin made of organized gangs

ALL: **including the cops**

I refuse to rot in this cesspool

B: I gave 'em $1.25 when it cost $1.50

Now the bus broke down

ALL: **I'm in the middle of downtown**

B: With an empty bus pass and a smile

ALL: **Let's hope they let me in for free**

B: I got to be at practice in a while

ALL: **Stand clear — the doors are closing**

K: Now I'm looking for a seat

I go to the back 'cause that's my habitat

ALL: **It's where I feel most comfortable**

K: Don't ask me to sit in the front

I feel like I'm being watched

Asking what drugs I got

ALL: **How many pills I popped**

to stay focused

K: 'Cause getting to poetry rehearsal

is my only way out

ALL: **Stand clear — the doors are closing**

W: I just passed Skid Row

and all I see is that 4-year-old

who clenched my mama's hand

ALL: **That rides this same damn train**

W: Seems like a shame but it isn't

'cause I'm on my way to practice

B: I was blessed with a rush in my bloodline

ALL: So quitting is a joke, not an answer
B: and this bus line represents
my drive to keep going
ALL: This city is beautiful
but we have to keep going
I love the people here
ALL: But we have to keep going
K: Like the lungs of a rehabilitated smoker
ALL: Graduation is getting closer
K: I'm too anxious to sit down
7th and Hoover is the next stop
I requested with every ounce
of energy
ALL: I gotta get it
K: For all the pills I popped
ALL: I gotta get it
K: For my brother getting robbed
ALL: I can't go back
K: But now the cops are getting on
ALL: Time for me to get off
ALL: Stand clear — the doors are opening
W: My past days were bad days
and doors were closing
ALL: Nobody noticed but me
W: So I had to make a change
Label myself a poet
Less nights are spent hungry
For college, I got a few options
All black universities
Less diversity

ALL: Doors are now open
W: because I was preserving
B: For a kid like me,
it was not likely
Now schools write me
ALL: letters of congratulation
You no longer have to live in the projects
The ghetto
The slum
B: Whatever you want to call it
Congratulations
The pen in your ear?
ALL: A weapon.
B: Your journal?
ALL: A gold mine.
B: Keep driving until the night falls
ALL: Just don't fall asleep on the Gold Line
W: Stand clear —
ALL: away from the negativity
B: Stand up —
ALL: don't fear the peer pressure
K: Stand tall—
ALL: be the building your ego jumps off of
We can't give up
Saying "what's the point of tomorrow?"
If we will never see our sunshine
Don't get us wrong
We love where we're from
but we cannot see our sons die
Stand clear —the doors are open.

ABOUT THE GET LIT PLAYERS

Marquesha Babers: After growing up homeless and channeling her pain into power, Marquesha has become a mentor for Get Lit and an ambassador for the film *Girl Rising*, which stresses the importance of education for girls in developing countries. With Get Lit, she has performed at the MUSE Conference in Oregon, at the Women in the World Summit at Lincoln Center (alongside Angelina Jolie and Hillary Clinton), at Cadogan Hall in London, and at colleges and universities throughout the nation. She has also appeared on the series *Verses and Flow*, and she is a blogger for ONE.org. Look out for her poetry anthology and memoir, coming soon to a bookstore near you!

Matt Beyer: Matt attended Harvard Westlake School in Los Angeles, and his favorite poet is E. E. Cummings. His hobbies include writing rap music with his best friends and learning as much new music as possible. He currently attends and plays baseball for Brown University in Rhode Island.

Hannah Dains: Hannah attends Harvard Westlake School, where her play *Concrete* was launched as a school-wide production in 2014. She placed as a semifinalist in the Blank Theater's Young Playwrights Festival, and she participated as a TEDx presenter on behalf of Sitka Performing Arts Camp. She loves poetry for its ability to connect disparate populations through universal experiences, and she's grateful to the Get Lit Players for this illuminating experience.

Belissa Escobedo: Belissa has performed at the NAACP Awards, the Hollywood Bowl, and the Library of Congress. She also cowrote the opening preamble to the United Nations' Global Goals. After graduating from LA County High School for the Arts (LACHSA), Belissa plans to attend drama school in the United Kingdom and work in theatre in London professionally.

Walter Finnie Jr.: After graduating from Youth Opportunities High School, Walter became the feature of a Youth Speaks short documentary called "The Drop-In," chronicling his amazing journey from a family that struggled with poverty and addiction to a scholarship at Lincoln University, the alma mater of his idol, iconic poet Langston Hughes. His poem "Stand Clear," written with Get Lit Players Brian Martinez and Kyland Turner, won the Raise Up Project, culminating in a performance at the John F. Kennedy Performing Arts Center in Washington, DC.

Raul Herrera: Raul Herrera is Get Lit's Lead Teaching Artist. After four years of performing across the country as a member of the Get Lit Players. He is now the coach to the program for which he once apprenticed, and he seeks to support at-risk youth in self-expression and confidence building. His stellar poetry garnered him an invitation to the White House.

He is a multi-gold medalist at the Phi Rho Pi National Championship for Speech & Debate and California's recipient of the Speech & Debate Pentathlon Award.

Khamal Iwuanyanwu: Khamal attends Cleveland Charter High School, where he actively participates in the Academic Decathlon. He was the highest scoring poet of Get Lit's 2015 Classic Slam for his poem "Sepia" a response to Sekou Sundiata's "Blink Your Eyes." He hosts an annual school fund-raiser at Cleveland called "COREchella," and he also serves as editor for the youth literary magazine *Calliope*. In 2015, Khamal performed his original poetry at the National Book Festival's poetry slam at the Library of Congress.

Ryan Jafar: Growing up with Bangladeshi parents has influenced Ryan's work as a poet and a rapper. He has channeled his childhood struggles into art—art that has carried him through high school, university, and beyond. He's been featured as a rapper and/or poet on CNN, NBC, the *Los Angeles Times*, HBO's *Brave New Voices*, and PBS's *Art & The Mind*. He now works as an MC and DJ all over Los Angeles.

Emily James: Emily attended El Rancho High School and now attends the University of California, Santa Barbara, majoring in film and media studies. At El Rancho High School, she served as captain of her high school's Academic Decathlon team, and copy editor and reporter for the school's newspaper, *El Rodeo*. Her work has been published in the *Los Angeles Times*, and she is an active advocate for the LGBT community.

Adrian Kljucec: Adrian graduated from Santa Monica High School and currently attends the University of Puget Sound in Washington State. He is a proud advocate for environmental rights and for the trans/queer community. He loves camping, nature, and theater, and he is honing his skills to become a professional actor upon graduation.

Ian Kohn: Ian attends the Humanities Magnet at Cleveland Charter High School. He is a powerful ambassador for community understanding of Asperger's syndrome, and he finds poetry a powerful mode of expression. In his words, "Poetry, I believe, is the main recourse a person can access when their true identity is being suppressed by the outside world." Other passions of Ian's include running and practicing Taekwondo.

Jamiah Lincoln: Jamiah attends El Camino Real Charter High School and is a proud member of the American Cancer Society photography committee. She holds a 3.3 GPA and serves in the cabinet for her El Camino Real's Black Student Union. She has performed at schools and political events all over LA, including Supervisor Mark Ridley-Thomas's Empowerment Congress with Dr. Cornel West, and at Dodger Stadium with Alan Ball. Her inspirations include Maya Angelou and Toni Morrison.

Maia Mayor: Maia is a graduate of Champs Charter High School and a three-year veteran Get Lit Player. While representing Get Lit, she has been featured on Pacifica Radio and Fox News; performed at the Actors' Gang, the Wiltern Theater, and colleges and universities throughout the nation. Maia has been a featured speaker and performer for TEDxYouth.

Rhiannon McGavin: After gaining recognition for her YouTube channel, the Geeky Blonde, Rhiannon has grown to use the platform as a collection of DIY projects, *Condensed Shakespeare* vignettes, and original poetry, as well as to advocate for global freedom from sex trafficking and cyberbullying. She has performed at Lincoln Center, the Hollywood Bowl, and the Library of Congress. She is a member of SoulPancake's Bridge Exchange to present poetry at film festivals, and she led Supervisor Mark Ridley-Thomas's 2014 March Against Sex Trafficking. Additionally, she cowrote the preamble for the United Nations' Global Goals for sustainable development. Follow her journey at thegeekyblonde.com.

Zachary Perlmuter: Zach is a proud graduate of John R. Wooden High School, and he helped coach Wooden's team all the way to finals at the 2015 Classic Slam! He is a muralist and an advocate for gang recovery and social activism through art. He performs poetry at high schools, colleges, and universities throughout California, and works as a Get Lit mentor, coaching elementary and high school students alike.

Jessica Romoff: A graduate of the California State Summer School for the Arts (CSSSA), Jessica is a student at Brentwood School, a California Arts Scholar, and member of Mayor Garcetti's Youth Policy Council to improve civic engagement by youth in Los Angeles. She represented Get Lit as a Youth Poet Laureate finalist, and she has received Benefacta status for her commitment to community service in LA.

Miriam Sachs: Growing up, Miriam found spoken word a natural love-child of her two great passions: theater and writing. She runs a monthly salon called In-House Arts in Manhattan Beach; she cofounded the creative writing club at Mira Costa High School; and she is the news director of her school's biweekly broadcast, the *Mustang Morning News*. She will attend USC film school in fall 2016.

Max Toubes: Max attends LACES Magnet School and is passionate about hip-hop music and culture (especially rap and street art), as well as guitar and music production. He currently works mentoring other teens in producing music with the Young Producers Group, and he creates his own electronic, hip-hop, and house music.

Kyland Turner: Kyland is passionate about social activism and has performed on *The Queen Latifah Show* where he received a $10,000 scholarship! Kyland has also performed for the Kennedy Center, the Entertainment Industry Foundation, the *Los Angeles Times* Festival of Books, and the White House. He was honored as an ABC "Cool Kid" for his work to improve academic engagement at his high school, and now attends Pasadena City College, where he studies sociology and performs in theatrical productions.

Diane Luby Lane is the founder and executive director of *Get Lit—Words Ignite*, a Los Angeles-based arts education nonprofit that is transforming the landscape of teen literacy by empowering new generations in literature, self-expression, and performing arts. She is also the founder of the *Get Lit Players*, an award-winning classic teen poetry troupe that has collaborated with the United Nations, Dove, and Women in the World, and toured at the Kennedy Center, Lincoln Center, and the White House, and more, igniting communities across the globe with art and social consciousness. Lane is also the founding producer of Get Lit's *Classic Slam*, the largest youth classic poetry festival in the world. Lane's *Lit Kit*, a standards based, in-school curriculum, has been adopted by schools throughout the U.S. and internationally, and Get Lit is an official partner of Turnaround Arts: California. She is the author of *Words of Women* (Samuel French) as well as the playwright and star of the critically acclaimed one-woman show *Deep Sea Diving* (also known as *Born Feet First*), which toured with iconic Chicano poet and author Jimmy Santiago Baca. Lane is a graduate of the Annenberg Foundation's Alchemy + Leadership Program, a TedX speaker, a Southern California Leadership Network Fellow, a member of Mayor Eric Garcetti's Poet Laureate Committee, and a recipient of the Presidential Lifetime Service Award. She lives in Los Angeles with her husband and two children.

Daniel Sawyer Schaefer: Daniel Sawyer Schaefer (photographer of the *Get Lit Rising* portraits) is a citizen of both coasts, splitting his time between Los Angeles and New York City, never without a camera slung at his side. After joining the Get Lit Players in 2010, his documentary-style photography and heavily narrative poetry began to flow together, each influencing the other greatly. Now working full-time as a professional photographer and television writer, there is no job he loves more than covering the Brave New Voices youth poetry tournament, where he follows the Get Lit Players and manages the still photography for the entire event. His work can be found at OutlierImagery.com and related social-media outlets. He now attends Columbia University.

If you have taken this rubble for my past
raking through it for fragments you could sell
know that I long ago moved on
deeper into the heart of the matter

If you think you can grasp me, think again:
my story flows in more than one direction
a delta springing from the river bed
with its five fingers spread.

                    —"Delta," Adrienne Rich

Join the LITERARY RIOT at getlit.org.

This book is dedicated to all the people who love us into being.

ACKNOWLEDGMENTS

So much goes into the creation of a book. So much goes into the creation of a person! I would like to thank all those who had a hand in both.

Thank you to all of the poets who are featured in this book. Your words, your stories, your generosity, your bravery, and your artistry live on, bringing texture and joy to the world. Most especially to Walt Whitman and Jimmy Santiago Baca for *Leaves of Grass* and *Healing Earthquakes*, from which I shall never recover.

Thank you to my best teachers and to the fate that brought you to me:

Viveca Lindfors for introducing me to Walt Whitman, poetry, and the "role that turns me inside out." Yours is the torch I carry in my heart.

James Kass for starting Youth Speaks, introducing me (and every young person in the world) to spoken word, and effectively altering the course of history.

Jimmy Santiago Baca for breathing books like I do. For taking my show on the road. Doors that were shut became open. I follow in your wake.

Thank you to Carol Muske-Dukes for your poetry and early support of our work.

Thank you Michelle Fiordaliso, the original editor of this manuscript—when it was just a collection of ideas. You are kind. And a genius. And thank you Daniel Schaefer (former Get Lit Player) for your beautiful photographs in this book!

Thank you to Fred Courtright for your help securing the permissions to the poems in this book. We truly could not have done this without you.

Thank you to my agent, Rita Rosenkranz, who helped me publish my first book nearly twenty years ago. Sometimes great (second) things take time!

To my mother—your humor, candor, and strength inspire. There is no one in the world I'd rather have a cup of tea with, dissect life with, and have for my mom. Like the saying says, "If you weren't my mother, you'd be my best friend."

Thank you to my magnificent siblings, Rich, Stephen, and Karen, you "Lucky Lubys" make me laugh more than anyone else in the world.

Thank you to our Get Lit staff (past and present)—and especially Amanda Pittman, Veronika Shulman, Paul Mabon, Raul Herrera, and Rachel Kilroy, all of whom I am beyond blessed to know.

Thank you to Get Lit board members (past and present), who have kept Get Lit growing and on the right track; all Get Lit volunteers; and Get Lit donors, whose generosity is behind all of the work that we have accomplished.

Thank you to our incredible family of Get Lit teaching artists, who change the chemistry of a class the minute they walk into a room.

Thank you to all of the Los Angeles County teachers who took a chance on this program and taught the Get Lit curriculum in their schools. You introduced me to many of the amazing poets featured in this book. You are the true heroes!

Thank you to all of my friends who helped me launch Get Lit, including Andrea and Michael Zomber, who produced my first show, which in a roundabout way, started Get Lit because it got me into the schools. Andrea—you've always had faith in the unseen. Thank you for believing in me. Your generosity changed my life. It created everything.

Jeffery Bihr—for recognizing *Deep Sea Diving* was a show about books and setting my story free.

Gary Stokoe—Leo friend, born the same day as my father. You have blessed me beyond measure. Even Rumi couldn't express all the thanks I have in my heart. Hafiz himself couldn't express all the love.

Karen Redman—most humble servant, smartest steward, laughing heart. You started as a $40 donor and ended up my best friend. I respect you more than anyone I have ever known.

Thank you to Get Lit partners like Tim Robbins at the Actors' Gang, Ed Pearl at the Ash Grove, Ned Colletti and the Los Angeles Dodgers, Malissa Feruzzi Shriver at Turnaround Arts, Phil and Monica Rosenthal, and all the many others. You make it a thrill to do this work.

Thank you to all Get Lit poets (past and present) and to their families. Watching you grow, graduate, succeed, and give back to the world is one of the great joys of my life. You have taught me so much and continue to keep me young/make me feel old all at the same time!

Thank you to our Los Angeles Poet Laureate, the iconic Luis Rodriguez, as well as Supervisor Mark Ridley-Thomas, Executive Director of Arts Education for Los Angeles Unified School District Rory Pullens, and Mayor Eric Garcetti for the projects we have worked on and all that you are doing to make Los Angeles great.

To Marianne Williamson for the inspiration that got me through my twenties and gave me the belief to start Get Lit in my thirties. You embody Goethe's words "The glory of God is man fully alive!"

To Tina Brown and Kyle Gibson for creating and producing the most unbelievable summit for women leaders in the world—Women in the World—and inviting our young poets to shine.

To my friends who have shared in this journey—most especially my dear soul sister, Jeanette Pavini; Jill Rosenthal; Heather Mathieson;

Stephanie Boye; Joelle Antico; Natalie Geld; Susanna Spies; Sabrina and Steve Weill; Michael Panes; Christine Spines; extended Luby and Lane families; plus all Orange Grove Groovers (past and present) and LCS Family.

The rocking James Catterall, whose reports got Get Lit taken seriously, and the indomitable Kim Zanti!

Brad Koepenick, for your vision and infectious spirit.

Jimmy Collins, for your beautiful videos that helped to tell our story.

Deb and Tom North—your early generosity kept us going! You exemplify all that is good in the world.

Thank you to Veronika Shulman for your trusted edits on this book, and especially the poems, and to Rachel Kilroy for tracking the permissions!

A giant thank-you to Simon & Schuster for publishing this book, and to Michelle McCann, Lindsay Brown, Emmalisa Sparrow, Whitney Diffenderfer, and everyone at Beyond Words for believing in this project and bringing it to life. It has been a great joy to work with all of you!

To my father, Richard Luby, for ears as large as conch shells. You are still the first person I want to call. And Catherine Luby for your friendship, and the journey we have shared.

And more than anyone or anything, and most especially, a special thank-you to my husband, Tim Lane. You have been with me every step of the way—with dinners, feedback, school pickups, every kind of support, and love. You inspire me every single day. I have never known a kinder human being... *and you're a cowboy*. Lucky me.

And finally, for Lukas and Millie: it's all for you and because of you. You are my heart.

CLASSIC POETRY CREDITS
(LISTED ALPHABETICALLY)

"Anthem"

Excerpted from *Stranger Music* by Leonard Cohen. Copyright © Leaonard Cohen. Reprinted by permission of McClelland & Stewart, a division of Penguin Random House Canada Limited.

"Barbie Doll"

From *Circles on the Water* by Marge Piercy, copyright © 1982 by Middlemarsh, Inc. Used by permission of Alfred A. Knopf, an imprint of the Knopf Doubleday Publishing Group, a division of Penguin Random House LLC. All rights reserved. Any third party use of this material, outside of this publication, is prohibited. Interested parties must apply directly to Penguin Random House LLC for permission.

"Blink Your Eyes"

By Sekou Sundiata. Reprinted with permission of Dance & Be Still Arts.

"Shout Out"

By Sekou Sundiata. Reprinted with permission of Dance & Be Still Arts.

"A Smile to Remember"

From *The Pleasures of the Damned* by Charles Bukowski. Copyright © 2007 by Linda Lee Bukowski. Reprinted by permission of Harper-Collins Publishers.

"Song No. 2"

Copyright © Sonia Sanchez from *Under a Soprano Sky*, (Trenton: Africa World Press, 1987).

"The Survivor"

Reprinted by permission from Anvil Press Poetry. Copyright © 1991 by Tadeusz Rózewicz from *They Came to See a Poet* published by Anvil Press Poetry. Translated by Adam Czerniawski

"Tonight in Yoga"

Reprinted by permission from Sierra DeMulder. Copyright © 2016 by Sierra DeMulder from *Today Means Amen* published by Andrews McMeel Publishing.

"Touched by an Angel"

Maya Angelou poem used with permission by Caged Bird Legacy, LLC.

"To You"

By Walt Whitman from *Leaves of Grass*, originally published in 1855.

"What Horror to Awake at Night"

Lorine Nidecker: Collected Works by Lorine Niedecker, edited by Jenny Penberthy, © 2002 by the Regents of the University of California. Published by the University of California Press.

"Women Want Fighters for Their Lovers"

From *The Complete Poems of D.H. Lawrence by D.H. Lawrence*, edited by Vivian de Sola Pinto and Warren F. Roberts, copyright © 1964, 1971 by Angelo Ravagli and C. M. Weekley, Executors of the Estate of Frieda Lawrence Ravagli. Used by permission of Viking Books, an imprint of Penguin Publishing Group, a division of Penguin Random House LLC.